MANAGING CHANGE IN THE EXCELLENT BANKS

Also by Steven I. Davis and published by Macmillan

THE EURO-BANK: Its Origins, Management and Outlook
THE MANAGEMENT OF INTERNATIONAL BANKS
EXCELLENCE IN BANKING

MANAGING CHANGE IN THE EXCELLENT BANKS

Steven I. Davis

St. Martin's Press   New York

All rights reserved. For information, write:
Scholarly and Reference Division,
St. Martin's Press, Inc., 175 Fifth Avenue,
New York, N.Y. 10010

First published in the United States of America in 1989

Printed in Great Britain

ISBN 0-312-03262-5

Library of Congress Cataloging-in-Publication Data
Davis, Steven I.
Managing change in the excellent banks/Steven I. Davis.
p.   cm.
Bibliography: p.
Includes indexes.
ISBN 0-312-03262-5: $19.95 (est.)
1. Bank management.   I. Title
HG1615.D4   1989
332.1'2068684—dc20

89-10141
CIP

To Joyce, Andrew, Christopher and Stephanie:
growing together

Contents

List of Tables

Preface

In the four years since *Excellence in Banking* was written, the pace of change in the banking world has accelerated. Journalists and consultants everywhere have been sustained by an outpouring of prose on the forces of globalization, securitization, deregulation and a host of other factors.

Amidst this tumult, readers of *Excellence in Banking* may understandably raise a number of questions. How have the excellent banks fared? How uniform are the pressures for change? Perhaps most important of all, what lessons do the banks at the firing line have for those advancing to the forward trenches?

My interest in picking up the pen – or rather a lap-top computer this time around – has been whetted by the positive response to *Excellence in Banking*, for which I am eternally grateful to Macmillan as well as the bankers who took the time to traverse it. It warmed this author's ego considerably not only to have the book translated into Japanese, Spanish, German and Portugese, but more importantly to see it on a number of senior bankers' desks with relevant quotations from their peers underlined and circled for future reference. The banking culture does indeed focus heavily on role models, but it was particularly satisfying to see experience transmitted through these pages.

In the meantime, my own perspective on the banking scene has been complemented by a broader array of management consulting assignments which have given me new perspectives on how banks are addressing the challenges of a ferociously competitive market. In a word, I have progressed from a neophyte banking consultant in 1984 to perhaps the adolescent stage. One of the more exciting of these assignments is to put on a financial analyst's hat for my good friend Tom Hanley of Salomon Brothers in New

York to review a number of major banking institutions in Europe and the Pacific Basin on an on-going basis.

As in 1984, the contribution of my panel of bank-watchers – or bankologists, to use the phrase of my partner Alan Banks – has been invaluable. Friends such as Dwight Crane at the Harvard Business School, John Rudy of Greenwich Research Associates, David Cates of Cates Consulting Analysts, Bill Turner of Price Waterhouse, and Robin Monro-Davies of IBCA Banking Analysis have contributed generously of their time and experience. Tim Farmiloe, my publisher, has been totally supportive as in the case of my previous literary labours. Dolores Mulroy has once again lent an essential hand – this time in introducing me to the mysteries of the PC.

But, as was the case in *Excellence in Banking*, it has all happened because of the willingness of so many bankers in 12 excellent institutions to take the time to reflect on their own experience in managing change. And even more, to share this with the competition. As one of my friends in a New York excellent bank commented in response to my request for yet more appointments,

> **one common thread in excellent bank management might be a focus on running the business rather than taking the time to talk about it. There is a low ROE in this competitive world in being a role model for peers.**

To which I can only say amen, – and thanks!

London   Steven I. Davis

Acknowledgements

Thanks are due to all the excellent managers who made this book possible.

The author and publishers acknowledge with thanks permission from the following to reproduce copyright material:

Salomon Brothers Inc. for data in Tables 1.1 and 10.1.
IBCA Banking Analysis for data in Tables 1.1 and 10.1.
DIBC for data in Tables 1.1 and 3.1.
Morgan Guaranty Trust for data in Table 10.1.
Morgan Stanley Capital International for data in Table 10.2.
McKinsey & Co. Inc. for Figure 4.1.

1 The Winds of Change

This book is about change in the banking world and how well-managed institutions have coped with it. Like its forerunner, *Excellence in Banking*, this volume attempts to identify common themes in successful management practice and synthesize them to enable bankers and bank watchers to spot winners and losers on the global banking battlefield.

Written in 1984, *Excellence in Banking* had two goals: first, to determine whether there was indeed such an animal as an excellent bank in the terminology of Messrs Waterman and Peters in their landmark volume *In Search of Excellence*. If so, what qualities did it have?

The second question was easier to answer. There are indeed common themes: a strong culture with well-defined values and open communications; consistent, strong and straightforward leadership; a check and balance approach to risk control; a commitment to lavishing resources on the care and feeding of superior people; and responsiveness to customer needs. Structure and management style, on the other hand, were wildly different, while few excellent institutions worried much about strategic planning.

But when stacked up against the paragons of *In Search of Excellence*, only one excellent bank – Citicorp – came close to the model. Innovation and experimentation are rare in a business where learning from others' mistakes is a virtue.

Excellence in Banking was, however, a static analysis in a world in the grip of massive change. One of the clear lessons from it was that the winds of change were indeed blowing through the sector, but they varied between a gentle breeze in Munich and Basel to gale force 10 in the canyons of Manhattan. Bankers in the former centers acknowledged to varying degrees that change was afoot, but assured themselves that the strength of core franchises would shelter them from the agonies to be suffered, for example, by the US money center banks.

An avalanche of change of Himalayan proportions has indeed descended upon bankers everywhere since 1984.

1

Deregulation has broken down product and geographic barriers as well as removed constraints on pricing in one country after another. Interstate banking has transformed the American banking landscape, while barriers in the capital market sector have been blasted apart by the Big Bang in London and similar explosions in Paris, Tokyo, Amsterdam and other markets. The combination in the US of legislative barriers against nationwide banking and the superior price earnings multiples of highly profitable state-wide institutions has produced in the US the phenomenon of superregional banks. These multistate powerhouses – assuming they can manage the merger process successfully – are mirroring the evolution in the 19th century of their forerunners in Europe and the Pacific basin which vaulted from regional to national leadership through acquisitions.

In national capital markets such as London and Paris, in which stockbroking and securities trading had been the province of specialist, lightly capitalized independent brokers, deregulation has taken the form of integration through acquisition of brokers by banking institutions intent on replicating the product lines of their European universal bank competitors. In the UK, for example, 19 of the 20 largest stockbrokers were acquired in the lead-up to 'Big Bang' in 1986.

Truly new products in the form of interest rate and currency swaps and their derivatives have exploded in a business which, as late as 1980, could comfort itself in the knowledge that product development was simply a matter of moving into other, existing financial products such as securities or insurance. The phenomenon of securitization – packaging loans for on-sale to investors – has swept the US market with the wave extending to the UK, where favourable economics and structural conditions had by 1988 created a £10 billion market in securitized home mortgage loans. The same tidal wave, moving from country to country in the 1980s, has also swept from bank balance sheets virtually all loans to borrowers who can fund more cheaply in the capital markets – essentially prime customers ranked 'A' and above by rating agencies. To replace these assets at least in part, banks have turned to higher yielding consumer lending (for those with the necessary network to capture retail loans) or to leveraged lending – financing changes in ownership for firms with a relatively modest equity base.

Having a solid customer franchise in the form of primary relationships with retail and unsophisticated corporate clients was indeed a boon, but without hitherto unprecedented investment in products, technology and human resources this franchise could disappear. Whereas the inflationary decade of the 1970s was characterized by ballooning personnel costs, the 1980s has been that of massive spending on information technology to link all dimensions of a bank's operations on a real-time basis so as to produce relevant management information, enable customers to access the bank's data base, and reduce unit operating costs.

For bankers and bankologists – that curious breed which devotes careers to the study of the banking genus – the obvious question is how banks – in particular the handful of excellent institutions under the microscope in *Excellence in Banking* – have fared under the storm clouds. In superficial terms, are they still excellent? How many angels have fallen or suffered bent haloes? In more substantive terms, how have the excellent banks dealt with the challenges of rapid change? Most important of all in a sector which more than most looks to role models, what lessons have been learned which could be useful to any bank addressing the same issues? And finally, what do these patterns of successful behavior foreshadow for an industry which is subject to more than its share of crystal ball gazing?

Cataclysmic predictions of the disappearance of the middle sized bank, the rise and fall of the global player, seismic shocks in the form of consolidation of weaker brethren – all are made on the basis of parallels with other industries undergoing change and deregulation, yet the experienced bankologist remarks that such change in practice seems to be less violent and more evolutionary when analyzed after the fact. The chemical, steel and airline industries in the US, for example, all have shed unproductive units and passed through a massive merger process to emerge leaner and more profitable. Is this the fate of banking? And finally, what of the Japanese threat? Sensitized in the US and Europe to the devastation of their electronics and automobile sectors by Japanese competitors investing for the long term in lower cost, higher quality products, non-Japanese bankers look with fear and trembling at their Japanese peers which benefit in addition from price/earnings ratios three to four times their own.

To answer these questions, the same methodology of *Excellence in Banking* has been put to work again. The international panel of 15 non-bank experts – career bankologists in effect – was resurrected to identify, without regard to their choices in 1984, an equivalent number of excellent institutions without regard to nationality, size, business profile or other criterion. With few exceptions – attributable to retirement and job change – this is the same group of transnational banking consultants, regulators, bank stock analysts and journalists which performed so ably in 1984. Up to two days was then spent with key executives in each institution focussing on two core questions: what do you regard as the key management issues facing your bank, and what lessons have you learned from addressing these issues? As in 1984, my interlocutors were the chief executive and senior executives with responsibility for the human resource, international, capital markets, risk, planning and other functions impacted most heavily by environmental change.

One casualty of change in banking has been the barrier between the securities and banking businesses. In *Excellence in Banking*, the focus was on institutions essentially engaged in the taking of deposits and lending of money. On this definition, British merchant banks such as S.G. Warburg were arbitrarily excluded. After Big Bang and similar explosions, it would have been naive to exclude securities companies from the book, so the panel was asked to include all financial institutions engaged primarily in the banking or securities businesses. Happily, S.G. Warburg now appears on the excellent list for *Managing Change in Excellent Banks*. Less happily, two of the three institutions selected by the panel but declining to participate in the book were securities companies.

The institutions which thus gained at least a significant minority of votes from the panelists are listed below:

Bankers Trust Company

Citicorp

Credit Suisse/CS First Boston

Deutsche Bank AG

First Wachovia Corporation

HongkongBank

J.P. Morgan and Co. Inc

National Westminster Bank Plc

PNC Financial Corporation (Pittsburgh National Bank)

Toronto Dominion Bank

Union Bank of Switzerland

S.G. Warburg Group

Eight of the 12 excellent banks – including the trio of Deutsche Bank, Morgan and Citicorp which won votes from virtually all the panelists in 1984 – thus returned in 1988. This time, however, only Morgan garnered almost all the panelists' votes. There were several switches: National Westminster replaced Barclays among the British candidates, while Credit Suisse (in association with its universally admired 45 per cent international investment banking affiliate CS First Boston) edged out its Swiss competitor Swiss Bank Corporation.

As one of our panelists put it:

There is still no truly international securities house except for CSFB.

S.G. Warburg joined the group on the basis of our new definition of banking institution. Finally, the ranks of the highly successful US superregionals produced PNC Financial Corporation to complete the dozen banks.

To quote one panelist:

PNC is a super-prime example of a bank that has acquisition/integration down to smooth poetry that has seduced every analyst and consultant.

Missing from the list are eight banks included in *Excellence in Banking*. Apart from the imprecision of the selection process

– an acknowledged weakness but not hopefully a critical one – what does this 50 per cent failure rate mean for the concept of an excellent banking institution? More importantly, can we relate it to the changes which are the subject of this book? Were any of our golden management rules broken by the fallen angels? Have the winds of change claimed victims already from the winners of 1984? More positively, what have the eight double winners done to stay in the race over the turbulent 1980s? There are a few satisfactory – and a number of less satisfying – answers to these questions. The most notable fall from grace was that of Texas Commerce Bank in Houston, whose asset quality problems had become evident when *Excellence in Banking* first appeared in print. Our panelists acknowledged that Texas Commerce was a victim of its home state's multiple problems – one panelist calls it 'environmental kill' – in the mid-1980s which have devastated all of TCB's peers to the extent that all of the seven largest Texas banks – including Texas Commerce – are now under new ownership. Yet the unanswered question is whether something else was involved – the credit process, cultural hubris, etc. Of more than hypothetical interest is the question of whether any banking institution with its franchise in Texas could have had the self-restraint and strong leadership in the early 1980s to turn away from energy and real estate lending. Only an exhaustive study – well beyond the limits of this book – could answer these questions in a responsible fashion. Suffice it to say that other excellent banks – including several described in this book – have put survival ahead of growth, scrupulously limited concentrations of risk, and emerged successfully from franchises which were collapsing around their ears.

There is a more generic response to the omission of most of the other banks. One of the panel's dilemmas has been to isolate the variable of management quality from others such as physical size and strength of domestic franchise. A New York money center bank struggling to build a new strategy in the wake of securitization is thus more easily put under the bankologist's microscope than a regional bank in Bavaria or a semi-deregulated City bank in Tokyo. How can one possibly compare the agonies of a Bankers Trust or J.P. Morgan in building – as its core business – a global securities capability almost from scratch with a Sumitomo Bank still enjoying a profitable, semi-sheltered domestic retail franchise? One senses a shift in the thinking of panelists – especially those from rating agencies who are acknowledging increasingly that ratings – often a product of physical size and therefore indispensibility to a national banking system – may or may not correlate well with management quality.

But one *can* relate in many cases perceived success in addressing core issues with the panelists' selections. The most notable fall from grace is the absence of the two Japanese banks from the current list. One, Bank of Tokyo, has regularly won kudos for quality of management, but its absence this time may reflect the bank's difficulty in an admittedly hostile environment in defending its traditional role as Japan's leading international bank. Its earnings performance has suffered from the burden of overseas problem loans, while other Japanese competitors have outdistanced it in the race to build a capital markets capability. Sumitomo Bank, on the other hand, seems to have suffered at least in the short term from two bold moves to position itself in a deregulated world: the acquisition of a non-voting minority interest in the leading New York investment bank Goldman Sachs and the domestic purchase of a troubled retail bank, Heiwa Sogo, to build market share in the buoyant Tokyo region. In the view of several in our panel, the jury is still out in the Sumitomo case: the financial burden of the Heiwa Sogo acquisition and the pyschological shock of not being able to use the Goldman Sachs investment as a springboard to global investment banking leadership may in ten years' time be seen to be the temporary ill effects of two brilliant strategic moves.

Pure statistical performance – the basis for most Anglo-Saxon panelists' recommendations – accounts for other ranking shifts. National Westminster Bank was beginning to overtake Barclays in most performance indicators when the panel voted in 1984, and relative performance since then has confirmed National Westminster – at least until now! – as the choice of analysts looking primarily at the numbers. By the same token, PNC's superlative profit performance in recent years has overshadowed that of Security Pacific and other US peers outside the money center ranks. Security Pacific received high marks again for its innovative approach to diversification, but our panelists were concerned about management's ability to pull these diverse elements together and have the patience to stay the course.

How do the 12 excellent banks in this volume stack up in terms of statistical performance against their peers? We asked this question in *Excellence in Banking*, and the response was, with a few exceptions, 'quite well'. This time around, we have a data base extending back to 1983, and the results for the eight institutions in both books should be particularly revealing.

Table 1.1 below provides for all the 12 banking institutions in this book comparative data for three critical performance measures over the 1983–88 period: after tax return on equity (ROE), after tax return on total assets (ROA) and annual compound growth in earnings per share. Where applicable, peer group performance is supplied by the relevant Salomon Brothers or DIBC composite.

As was the case in *Excellence in Banking*, the data in Figure 1.1 show, by and large, an above average statistical performance. Toronto Dominion, PNC Financial, S.G. Warburg and First Wachovia have clearly outperformed their rivals on all criteria since 1983 where peer group data is available. All of the banks except National Westminster and Deutsche Bank have demonstrated superior earnings growth, while the US money centre banks in 1988 lagged their composite only because of non-operating income reported by some of their peers. HongkongBank has shown declining returns on assets and equity but a steady growth in reported earnings, while S.G. Warburg, which continues to maintain hidden reserves in its merchant banking business, is widely acknowledged to be outperforming its British rivals. Deutsche Bank's performance over the 1983–88 period suffers in comparison to its competitors' earnings recovery since the lows reached in the early 1980s, but its record is generally regarded as superior in most performance measures.

In aggregate terms, all but one of the banks boasted an increase over the six year period in earnings per share. Ten of the 12 actually produced an increase in ROA between 1983 and 1988 on this basis, while eight sported higher returns on equity in 1988. On balance, not bad during a period of transition and change.

TABLE 1.1   Performance comparisons of excellent banks, 1983–8

Banking Institution Peer Group	Return on Equity 1983	1988	Return on Assets[2] 1983	1988	Earnings per Share compound annual growth: 1983–88
A **US money center banks**					
*Bankers Trust	15.5%	20.3[1]	0.67%	1.12%[1]	14.0%[1]
*Citicorp	16.0	20.5[1]	0.67[1]	(0.90)[1]	10.6%[1]
*J.P. Morgan	14.8	18.5[1]	0.79	1.21[1]	15.4%[1]
–Salomon Bros composite	14.3	21.6	0.64	1.04	9.6
B **US regional banks**					
*First Wachovia	18.7	17.2[1]	1.12	1.22[1]	11.0[1]
*PNC Financial	15.7	19.0[1]	1.02	1.20[1]	16.3[1]
–Salomon Bros composite	13.2	15.1	0.69%	0.83	7.2
C **Canadian banks**					
*Toronto Dominion	19.7	20.0[1]	0.74	1.15[1]	15.9%[1]
DIBC Canadian composite	NA	17.2	NA	NA	15.4
D **German banks[3]**					
*Deutsche Bank	9.7	6.3[1]	0.33	0.28[1]	(4.1)[1]
–Salomon Bros composite	8.7	7.5[1]	0.26	0.27[1]	2.4[1]
E **British banks**					
*National Westminster	14.6	18.8	0.76	1.12	(8.7)
–Salomon Bros composite	11.3	(18.7)	0.62	(1.11)	12.3

TABLE 1.1   (*continued*)

Banking Institution Peer Group	Return on Equity		Return on Assets[2]		Earnings per Share compound annual growth: 1983–88
	1983	1988	1983	1988	
F					
Swiss banks[3]					
*Credit Suisse	7.2	8.6	0.47	0.61	6.3
*Union Bank of Switzerland	8.9	7.8	0.46	0.53	6.2
–Salomon Bros. composite	8.2	8.0	0.45	0.55	5.4
G					
Hongkong Bank[3]	14.4	12.7	0.79	0.58	10.0
H					
S.G. Warburg group	14.8	15.4[1]	1.30	1.69[1]	18.6[1]
DIBC UK merchant bank composite	13.8	12.1	0.79	1.06	NA

Sources: Salomon Brothers; IBCA Banking Analysis; DIBC.
Notes:
1   1987 data; 1988 data not available at time of publication.
2   For banks in U.K. and Switzerland, figure of earning assets is used.
3   Data for German, Swiss banks and HongkongBank is based on disclosed net income which considerably understates reality on a US accounting basis.
    NR = Not relevant; NA = Not Available.

What conclusions can be drawn from the statistics? Basically that perceived management excellence is only partially reflected in the bottom line numbers at a single point in time. The level of profits from a relatively sheltered franchise is clearly a vital consideration. A European bank's lucrative national retail business provides a support which is not available to an excellent New York City money center bank like Citibank or J.P. Morgan which is deploying its excellence in building new businesses. Variables such as the extent of hidden earnings and assets, different policies of reserving against problem country loans and other factors also cloud the picture. More important, however, is the need to take a long term view in an industry where the pace of change differs from market to market. In this context, it is gratifying to see how many excellent institutions continue to produce healthy returns to their shareholders.

Of most significance to the author, however, is the continued – and in some cases increased – confidence of the panel in the quality of management of most of the banks selected in 1984. We emphasized repeatedly in *Excellence in Banking* that there was no magic to the selection process or the individual banks selected. Our goal then – and now – was to extract traits of excellent management practice from the experience of a reasonably wide range of banks generally perceived to be outstanding performers. The big vote winners of 1984 are still the stars of 1988. As one panelist puts it:

The good ones have shown bottle. I'm more confident with the present list.

Dissecting the reasons for attrition between the two dates is worthy of a volume of its own. One factor – most evident in the case of Texas Commerce and to a lesser extent, Barclays in the early 1980s – is the relative failure of risk control measures – the subject of Chapter 9 in *Excellence in Banking*. Another is certainly the difficulty of identifying and implementing a competitive strategy – the subject of Chapter 6 in the present volume. Skandinaviska Enskilda Banken, Security Pacific Corporation, and Bayerische Vereinsbank all continue to prosper in their domestic markets, yet their success outside traditional markets – the subject of Chapter 3 in this volume

– has evidently not impressed our panel to the extent of that of institutions such as Bankers Trust and J.P. Morgan.

In sum, we believe the traits of excellence remain those described in *Excellence in Banking*. The challenge of this book is to relate them to the changes sweeping the banking world.

To address this challenge, each of the excellent bankers interviewed was asked to identify the management issues he or she viewed as the most important facing their institution and to summarize the lessons of experience in dealing with these issues. After only a few days of interviews, the title of the book emerged with total clarity. One senior banker after another pointed out that all of the issues on the table related to change. In the halcyon days of a fully regulated banking sector, banks could be administered according to an established rule book. Today, management is increasingly regarded as the distinguishing feature between winners and losers in an overcrowded business.

Having identified the common thread linking the core issues, it remained to select the key issues themselves – those within management's purview which were central to top management's concerns for the future. Five such issues fitted this description, and each of Chapters 2–6 in the book will address one of these issues. Some, such as risk and technology, were examined in a different context in *Excellence in Banking*. Others, such as geographic and product expansion and the management of different cultures, have since been posed by the oft-repeated challenges of deregulation, securitization, and globalization of the banking business.

Chapters 7–10 of the book will then address what the author regards as the ultimate role of the bankologist – to identify the critical success factors in today's changing banking environment. How important are capital and other measurements of physical size? How can one probe beyond the tirelessly reiterated statement that 'we're in a people business'? What, in effect, will separate winners from losers in the 1990s?

Such a prototype of the excellent banking institution is also an amalgam of themes covered elsewhere in the two books, such as superior human resources and a realistic strategy. It also speaks to oft-articulated but little defined parameters such as critical mass. Most important of all, these chapters will examine in some detail how the excellent banks actually implement in practice these worthy standards of excellence. Chapter 10 pulls the strands of the book together in the content of strategic positioning. Its goal is to portray — at least from the author's crystal ball — some sense of the banking landscape of the future.

Finally, Chapter 11 revisits *Excellence in Banking* in the light of the findings of this book to test the conclusions of the first book with specific reference to the changes which have taken place in the two excellent lists between 1984 and 1988. Its goal is to inspect the individual choices of our panel and relate them to our four success factors, as well as to developments in the banking world since the first book was written.

Like its predecessor, this volume will be studded with direct quotations from successful bankers. Throughout the process of distilling notes from dozens of interviews, the author has found once again that the practitioners can generally articulate reality much better than he.

2 Risk: Some New Dimensions

We've relearned that the more exotic the product, the higher the risk you run if you don't take the trouble to understand the risk. – Tom Jones, Citicorp.

As befits an industry built on risk assessment, the issue of risk is at the forefront of the concerns of the excellent banks. Whereas the focus of risk in *Excellence in Banking* was on strategies to manage risk in the traditional commercial banking loan products, it is now on two quite different challenges. Firstly, the advent in the early 1980s of the wholly new array of rate risk management products such as interest rate swaps has posed challenges of product understanding and control. Secondly, replacing prime loans lost to securitization with Leveraged Buyouts (LBO) and other so-called leveraged products raises not only issues of risk reward but also one of strategic choice for those not prepared to accept the risks of corporate lending as defined in the late 1980s.

While controlling interest rate and currency risk through swaps burst on the international banking scene in 1982, six years later these and other related products are still regarded by most practitioners as 'new'. Bill Brock, Executive Vice President of credit for Toronto Dominion expresses a typical view:

Swaps are brand new. There's no old product to modify. That's the terrorizing aspect. On top of that, the products have a short life cycle. First, we need to understand the risk. Then we need the accounting systems to control it – but in most banks they aren't yet in place.

In such an environment, with the product specialist driven by the often substantial profits to be gained by grasping market opportunities, management and control systems can be left far behind. Bob Engel, formerly head of J.P.

14

Morgan's corporate banking function and now Group Executive responsible for strategic development, describes the management dilemma:

> **You have to make sure the creative people are tracked – that the cart doesn't get too far in front of the horse. There has to be a blend of product cycle and back office requirements.**

Intertwined with this issue is the difficulty of many top managers in understanding risks which require a high degree of numeracy as well as at least a superficial understanding of complex valuation models. To quote Joe Manganello, head of credit at Bankers Trust, one of the leaders in the risk management business:

> **There are three areas of risk which have become increasingly interrelated: counterparty risk (which is more complex than it used to be), market or rate risk and liquidity risk. There's an obvious need for information on a very real time basis. The process for putting risk on the books hasn't changed much, but the monitoring process is more complex. The issue is what kind of tiger you have by the tail. It's a major effort here. What helps us a lot is our own new product review process. Before you deal in a new product, a credit officer has to intervene, and he can say 'I don't understand this product'. We proceed only after we're comfortable with the risk and know how we're going to monitor it.**

At Citicorp, Chairman John Reed acknowledges the unknowns involved:

> **We spend a lot of the time with the mathematics trying to understand some of these new products. It is very complicated stuff, and there is an uncertainty principle much as in physics, where there are some things you will never know until they happen.[1]**

All of the excellent banks agree that top management must understand the risks of the new products. Hans-Joerg Rudloff, Chief Executive of Financiére Credit Suisse – First Boston and one of the leading figures in the international securities business, summarizes the dilemma:

> We basically dissect, sell or swap cash flows. If there's
> a steep Deutsche mark yield curve, there's a lot of
> potential in splitting it up. But you have to develop
> the accounting procedures. Your people say 'We're
> hedged'. So management sleeps well – until there's a
> dramatic change like October 1987. The big risk isn't
> volatility – it's using theoretical values. Modern theo-
> ry says that you value an option on a widely used
> valuation model. So banks start to write options valued
> on that model. But if you have to sell, other people
> may think totally differently. In a forced liquidation
> the value is what someone is willing to pay.

A typical management response to this challenge is that of
Charles Baillie, Executive Vice President of the treasury and
investment banking function of Toronto Dominion, which is
a relatively late arrival on the rate risk management front.

> My biggest worry is that I find out we've lost money
> because we didn't understand a product. We're doing
> a good job but there's a rapid rate of change. If we
> can't understand it, we don't do it. We have the comp-
> troller and the other experts go through and explain
> the risks. They have to satisfy me. We look at the
> historical volatility and figure out what you could
> lose. Can we get out; is there a liquid market, or is
> it a dream. What is the worst case? If I'm not totally
> comfortable, we might establish a small limit.

Complicating management's task is the tension injected by
incentive compensation. Recruited and trained to generate
profits from innovative techniques, rate risk management
specialists are often compensated largely on the basis of
direct profit contribution. Tom Jones, Senior Corporate
Officer and head of the financial control function of Citicorp,
puts it neatly:

> We've relearned that the more exotic the product, the
> higher the risk you run if you don't take the trouble to
> understand the risk. You can't have the trader valuing
> the position. If it's that difficult to measure the position,
> then restrict the volume. The dilemma is that when
> it's hardest to measure profit you can probably make

the most money. There's a creative tension with the accounting function. We hadn't realized four years ago how much discipline was lacking in investment banking. We have faith in our risk management system but we're constantly evaluating it.

So how does management resolve the dilemma of vast potential profits in an innovative sector but equally vast potential for loss? The universal response from all the excellent banks is to use subjective judgement. Larry Glenn, Citicorp's Chairman of the Credit Policy Committee, speaks for many of his peers:

> There are all the appearances in banking of dramatic change, but the fundamentals don't change. On rate risk management products, it all comes down to 'T' accounts – getting the elements in the right brackets. It's funny how only the most experienced bankers think in these simple terms. Secondly, you can get a bright PhD in mathematics to build a statistical model, but you had better be able to understand the ramifications of the methodology and to balance it with judgement. Turning it over to the technicians is the risk. It scares me to death.

Another guideline is self-discipline: the commitment to live with proven control techniques, starting slowly with tight limits in a new product and looking at worst case scenarios. Larry Glenn continues:

> Can you have the same trusting style? Controlling foreign exchange is easy, but as you move into a more subjective universe, things get tougher. We get our head handed to us every time we say to a trader 'you value it'. You need the self-discipline to follow precepts – clear cut rules on how to manage dealers.

J.P. Morgan is another pace-setter in risk management products, and the message is the same: use your judgement to run the book. Walter Gubert, Morgan's head of securities in London, summarizes his approach:

> Analytical models can be great, but don't let the people who build the model make the decisions. You have to see *beyond* the model: It's a tool, not the

answer. Don't let the quants run your trading book. It's a question of judgement.

For some of the excellent banks – quite apart from the banking universe in general – the risks of the new arbitrage products outweigh the benefits. First Wachovia is not a user of them. Hans Geiger, the member of the Executive Board of Credit Suisse with responsibility for the foreign exchange and money market function, summarizes a typical view:

> **There isn't a new dimension of risk. Over the years there have been a lot of risks we haven't understood – so we don't do the deal. We don't run a large option book as a result. You have to understand your business. I am intellectually fascinated by the concept of dynamic hedging. But what happens if you don't have a market?**

Any difference in views among the excellent banks on rate risk management is dwarfed by the split produced by the explosive growth of leveraged lending. All can agree on the background to the issue: the process of securitization which has swept from banks' balance sheets virtually all loans to rated – say 'A' and above in the US rating parlance – borrowers. The wave of securitization has spread to Japan, the UK, France, Germany, Spain and a variety of other national markets, leaving banks with the strategic choice of exiting the corporate lending business, moving down market to lesser rated middle market borrowers, or participating in the leveraged lending sector. Originating in the US leveraged buyout business, this now encompasses management buyouts, development capital, mezzanine finance and so-called bridge finance. The debate is an intense one.

Bankers Trust is a leader in the leveraged lending business, and Joe Manganello puts the positive case:

> **Assessing risk in leveraged lending isn't very different. You're still looking at management quality, cash flow, asset quality and vulnerability to various economic cycles. But you're looking at them against a more highly leveraged balance sheet.**
>
> **The key is not to be over-optimistic about the growth of earnings and to have a broadly diversified portfolio.**

Another positive view is articulated by Larry Glenn of Citicorp:

> There's no question that incremental leverage adds incremental risk. But historically the biggest losses have been unsecured credits. The more structured the credit, the less risky it's likely to be. Management knows it has to react if there's a problem. Essentially we've already negotiated the workout, and if we hit problems, change comes very fast.

Most of the excellent banks, however, are much less sanguine about the likely losses to be suffered in leveraged lending. The impact of unfavorable economic conditions on the reduced equity cushion, the large size of individual transactions, the difficulty in realizing asset values – all lead some excellent bankers to the conclusion that leveraged lending will be the banking graveyard of the 1990s as LDC lending was in the 1980s and real estate finance in the 1970s.

First Wachovia has always placed survival and soundness above profit growth, and Bud Baker, Executive Vice President and head of the merged banks' credit function, articulates the concerns of a conservative lender:

> It's an issue of balance. Sound portfolio management requires balance in the decision-making process and in the kinds of risk you can take. Banks are extending credit in a time of great change. Fads appear regularly, are chased by banks and disappear quickly. We still believe in customer relationships which are of a longer term nature. This may cause us to be less interested in speculative transactions and may cause our loan growth to slow in highly volatile periods. We may have to suffer a bit in the short run.

> In recent years we have helped our customers to find new ways to become indebted. As a result loans have grown faster than the national economy. Ultimately this will have to come back into balance. It is not lost on me that I ran International for seven years and that we charged off in 1988 more on LDC loans than I ever earned for the bank in that position.

The corporate lender's anguish is echoed at Toronto Dominion, a skilled lender which prides itself on its expertise in evaluating complex credits. Bill Brock articulates both the strategic and risk/reward dilemmas:

> **It raises the question of the kind of bank you want to be, because the average level of risk in the portfolio will rise. In retrospect we made a mistake in the 1970s to allow the LDC loans to become a disproportionate part of our business. LBO risks are different: we're essentially transferring middle market lending expertise to major corporates. Normally in our experience about two out of 300 credits go on non-accrual; if we get any higher ratio in our portfolio, then we've got a problem.**

For the excellent banks struggling with this risk/reward dilemma, an additional complication is the high average size of loan participation in the typical leveraged buyout. As Bud Baker of First Wachovia puts it:

> **It's fascinating historically to see how credit losses have detracted from earnings growth in banking. We're reaching the point where banks can't afford to take the significant losses that may lie ahead. The entry fee for an LBO loan may be $100 million. It's very sobering to contemplate a $100 million workout.**

A new dimension introduced by leveraged lending is the good news of securitization: some of these loans can be marketed to other banks or third party investors. For banks like Bankers Trust and Citicorp with the marketing apparatus to sell off these loans, the risk/reward ratio can be transformed – in their favor – by earning extra front end fees and reducing net exposure. Joe Manganello of Bankers Trust explains their portfolio approach to risk management:

> **One out of 100 LBO loans may well go wrong. The answer is portfolio management and limits on concentration. We do our analysis on risk concentration and sell down as appropriate through the distribution function. If we do take a hit, it will be one that we can absorb.**

As in the case of other debates over credit quality, this one will be resolved only over time as repayment schedules on LBO lending are met – or not. Skeptics abound outside the circle of US money center banks which are driving the business. A typical response from one of the excellent Swiss or German banks indicates a cautious, tentative approach to the business. A typical view is that of Rudolf Hug, a member of the Executive Board at Credit Suisse:

> **We've invested lots of time in acquiring the know-how, but we are very reluctant to do LBOs. We're convinced that at the end things will come home to roost. There's a philosophical question too: is value being created? Perhaps it's the opposite: they're selling off the best parts. Basically the risk/reward doesn't make sense.**

Perhaps the most balanced – and open – analysis from the standpoint of a senior lending officer is that of George Davis, Citicorp's head of North American banking and a Group Executive:

> **In our business [corporate finance] there's gross over-capacity – too much money chasing too few deals. The average top quality asset on our books may be rated BB. We underwrite huge sums to do a deal. The product line has changed: 50% of my business today is deals – with potentially a highly variable income stream. I think it will continue, but maybe not at the same rate. Deal risk has a variety of new dimensions. First, we're now in the securities business, which means whatever we do, we sell. There is now a due diligence risk in addition to credit risk. Our average asset is of lesser quality, so losses will rise – but our losses to date are less than for the rest of our business. It's OK if we get paid for the risk, but overcapacity hurts. In our LBO business we think it's properly done, but we won't know for sure until we are tested by recession.**

One means of bringing the two disparate views together is to develop a relative measure of risk. Well before the Cooke Committee of the Bank for International Settlements established guidelines for capital to be assigned to different on- and off-balance sheet assets, Bankers Trust had evolved its well known RAROC – risk adjusted return on capital –

formula. RAROC reduces relative risk to a single percentage figure which incorporates time (in the form of duration – the weighted exposure period), perceived counterpart risk and relative claim on capital. Joe Manganello explains:

> **It's relatively simple. Each risk asset type is categorized: 1 to 4 for investment grade, 5 to 9 for others. The formula shows how much capital is needed, and you match that with the expected return. It doesn't identify in an empirical way the bad credit, but you can compare the risk/reward trade-off.**

But the skeptics abound. Looking at all the developments in the banking world since *Excellence in Banking* was written, Dick Thomson, Chairman and Chief Executive Officer of Toronto Dominion, sums up the view of the chief executive:

> **The big change has been the growth of no-equity deals in New York. It has all the earmarks of LDC lending. It may be the new 'tulip' phase [of rampant speculation followed by panic] – a kind of dream world where you don't need equity. We're very conservative but running scared. It's like playing with fire. Banks should never get into a situation where they *have* to do the business.**

In conclusion, banking is still largely about risk. The risk profile has evolved with the changing environment – rate risk management as interest rate, currency and other variables fluctuate wildly in a deregulated world, and leveraged finance as banks struggle to apply their basic credit skills to a dwindling band of corporate borrowers which cannot find alternative finance. The guidelines articulated in *Excellence in Banking* still hold true: avoid risk concentrations, understand the risks, and proceed with due caution in a check-and-balance decision-making structure.

Yet the strategic issues are clearer now than in the early 1980s. The risk/reward ratio in the core lending businessess throughout the world continues to deteriorate. Even the advent in 1988 of globally-accepted minimum capital requirements for risk assets – like so many earlier events which were supposed to equilibrate the supply and demand for earning assets at rates which produced an acceptable yield for lenders – has failed to arrest the decay. Bankers who have waited impatiently since the early 1970s for acceptable yields on desirable lending assets have had to acknowledge an apparently structural oversupply of willing lenders. Retail lending in the 1980s has been a boon to banks able to generate the business. Yet arguably this saving grace has been a one-off adjustment of consumer borrowing and habits fostered by a happy combination of falling interest rates, sustained growth in personel incomes and an awakening of retail banks to the unexploited borrowing potential of their customer deposit base.

Whatever the evolution of future risk/reward ratios and the outcome of the great debate over leveraged lending, excellent banks the world over are confronted with a strategic dilemma: How much reliance can be placed in the future on lending – in any form – as a business? As subsequent chapters will indicate, the answers are not reassuring.

3 Geographic and Product Expansion: Building a New Franchise

It is in our national character to want to teach others to be Swiss. We're not the center of the world. – William Wirth, Credit Suisse.

A universal challenge for the excellent banks is to extend their reach outside their traditional franchise on a profitable basis. The negative argument for such an extension can be heard in almost every language spoken in the banking world: 'we've achieved the limits of market share expansion in our domestic market, margins are under pressure from competition and rising costs so we have to look to new markets'. A more positive motivation is expressed by banking institutions with product capability in a global or at least international market: 'unless we extend our reach abroad, we can't be competitive with those who are'.

The financial performance of the first category of banks – those looking to replicate a traditional banking business in a different geographic market – has not been overwhelming. Major US banks achieved attractive beachheads in European corporate banking business in the 1960s on the back of innovative product leadership in sectors such as cash flow lending and marginal cost pricing. The decade of the 1980s, however, has been marked by their retreat in the wake of aggressive responses by local peers. One of the fascinating ironies for the bankologist is that the buyers of these American-owned wholesale European banking branches in the late 1980s have been the new breed of international banks: institutions from Mediterranean and other countries looking – 20 years later – to build an international capability for the single European market projected for 1992.

24

The available statistical data on overseas profitability is fragmentary at best, but the mosaic of evidence in traditional corporate banking is depressing. Much more relevant in an age of scarce capital is their share of banking profits in overseas markets. Table 3.1 provides a profile of key performance data in those national markets where such data is available: Spain, France and Japan. Foreign banks as a whole have been able to command less than 10 per cent of the domestic lending market in most major OECD countries with a smaller share of lucrative core deposits.

The reasons for this uninspiring performance are depressingly familiar – and standard, whatever country is under the microscope. In a word, the local banks have got their act in order. They have invested in competitive information systems, trained their people in the latest products and marketing techniques, restructured their branch networks to offer a more cost-effective service and recruited back many local star performers who had joined leading US

TABLE 3.1   Foreign banks' share
of total bank lending and
earnings in selected countries, 1987 year-end

	Japan	Spain	France
Foreign banks' share of customers loans by all banks	0.9%[1]	14.4%[2]	10.4%
Foreign banks' share of all banks operating profits	0.4%[1]	10.3%	12.2%[4]
Foreign banks' operating profit[3] as % of total assets (ROA)	0.08%[1]	0.46%	0.31%[4]

Source: DIBC.
Notes:
1   Data for all foreign branches; year ended 31 March 1987.
2   Share of total banking assets.
3   Taken before income tax and special items.
4   Data for 1986.
c

money center banks in the 1960s and 1970s to learn the banking business from the industry's leaders.

The result in the late 1980s is global anguish for foreign banks looking for pure geographic expansion without a significant product advantage. Whether the market is Australia, Japan, Italy or Germany, foreign banks are increasingly groping for some form of product or other advantage – euphemistically known in the trade as niche banking. These efforts are led by the highly profit-sensitive US banks who are prepared to employ drastic surgery to restore profits.

But there *have* been successful geographic expansion strategies, and this chapter will attempt to scrutinize the reasons for their success. One such strategy is acquiring local businesses with a desirable client franchise, and the other is a product-driven strategy led by a well-defined superiority in a given product segment.

One of the generic conclusions reached by the excellent banks after decades of efforts to grow internationally is the durability of local resistance to penetration by outsiders – in particular foreign banks who may or may not have the requisite cultural sensitivity. Dick Thomson of Toronto Dominion makes the point from the standpoint of the defenders:

> **Banking at the regional level is a very local business. It's serving the public, and we've gone to great lengths to make it a local business. It frightens people to think that outsiders will make decisions [on their finances].**

The fragmentary evidence available suggests that foreign banks attacking new markets have had little success in garnering core, or principal, relationships with either retail, small corporate or even larger corporate customers. With these primary relationships go the lucrative deposit and daily transaction business which is the bread and butter of banking profits. Citicorp, the acknowledged industry leader in direct expansion into new geographic markets, has achieved impressive results in marketing individual retail products such as credit cards and mortgage loans across state lines in the US and in other markets such as Australia, Spain and Japan. Yet, profitable though these products may be in themselves, Citicorp in most markets where it does not have a retail branch network is still some way from capturing the client's primary banking relationship.

Felipe Oriol, Citicorp's Division Executive with responsibility for Spain, describes what happened following a major acquisition in the Spanish market:

> **In 1983 we bought a consumer banking vehicle. We developed a significant share of the car and home mortgage sectors and will double the network from 100 to 200 branches. From a profit standpoint, we're now [1988] just getting out of the investment period. We've built a limited but highly focussed product range, but we're still a second bank to our clients. Eventually we'll become the full relationship bank.**

The corollary of this recognition is a widespread humility on the part of aggressor banks with regard to the value they can add to running a banking business – particularly a retail one – in another market. Tom Frost, who ran National Westminster's US acquisition in New York before becoming the Group's Chief Executive Officer, speaks from direct experience:

> **What we bring to the party are the ability to pick well, to control properly and to keep our fingers on – or off – the business as appropriate. We make sure the target company is what we think it is. Foreign nationals can't properly run an indigenous bank. I did my job in a finite period, but my most important jobs were to get my successor in place and to impart our vision to North American management. We're not crawling over this business; we control it by the planning process.**

This view echoes throughout the ranks of the excellent institutions. The Swiss banks in particular are aware of their limitations in managing overseas businesses. William Wirth, member of the Executive Board and head of Credit Suisse's investment management function, makes the point in blunt terms:

> **Globalization means you have to go abroad, and the more you do so, the more you have to adapt to local rules. We can't impose ourselves simply because we're**

> **Swiss. It is in our national character to want to teach others to be Swiss. But we're not the center of the world; we have to adapt ourselves.**

His peers at Union Bank of Switzerland agree. Bruno Gehrig, a UBS Senior Vice President and head of securities, sales and trading world-wide, points out that:

> **Of course, you need a centralized system of risk controls. But to a certain extent you play according to the local rules. You can't say 'We are UBS'. We have a regional management in the UK which does what has to be done. It has to be assigned important responsibilities. We're moving in the direction of solving the management problem more and more on a regional level. It makes a hell of a lot of sense to delegate authority to the regions.**

The cultural gaps which underpin such resistance to change understandably vary widely from country to country. Delegation is an easier solution, say, between two Anglo-Saxon cultures than between an Anglo-Saxon and Latin or Asian one. Given the agreed need to delegate, the willingness to enter a new market is often a function of the perceived cultural gap. John Melbourn, Chief Executive of National Westminster's Corporate and Institutional banking business and former Head of International Banking, expresses a common view:

> **There's a world of difference between doing business in Cheltenham [UK] and Yonkers [NY]. You need to be seen to be part of the community. A German bank likes clearly defined guidelines, whereas you have to be very flexible in Italy.**

While there is little doubt about the sincerity of head office management's intellectual commitment to local delegation, the bankologist senses a certain ambivalence between talk and action. What a consulting friend calls a national institution's 'cultural baggage' must weigh considerably in the reality of day-to-day management. Guido Hanselmann, an Executive Vice President and senior planning officer of Union Bank of Switzerland and formerly head of the international sector, expresses a common approach which attempts to take the best of two worlds:

The secret is a successful marriage between two cultures. We have excellent senior Japanese staff in Tokyo, and in New York we've put all our activities into one building so they have to rub shoulders all the time. Foreigners should get the UBS culture as soon as possible. Some people in NY are more UBS -minded than in Zurich. The precondition is that Swiss staff also know what the real world outside Switzerland looks like.

It is to Citicorp to whom the excellent banks turn as a role model for a truly multinational approach to national markets. In country after country, Citi's success is cited as the closest approximation to the ideal of a global meritocracy. Tom Jones, a Briton who as Senior Corporate Officer is one of the principal non-US officers of Citicorp, articulates the strategy:

You can't be seen to be a US bank with a local presence. You need a senior local officer. The network means something to local customers. You need corporate disciplines, such as controls and ethics. And it costs money – to give the service the customer needs.

Another senior non-US career Citicorp banker, Victor Menezes, a Senior Corporate Officer who has responsibility for strategic planning, adds:

The key is a true commitment to decentralization; we run it abroad almost to a dysfunctional degree. The guy in Hong Kong makes decisions and is accountable for them. Without it, you can't build good cadres. We have 90 people running 90 different banks abroad in different environments.

The global – or at least transnational – nature of many product markets is both a challenge and an opportunity for many excellent banks in the battle to expand abroad. Some businesses have become truly global: investment management, foreign exchange, certain fixed interest markets such as US treasuries, and a number of rate risk management products. Others, like leveraged lending and mergers and acquisitions, offer opportunities to the practitioner with domestic expertise under his belt.

For many excellent banks, however, there is an acute awareness that their domestic capabilities add little value abroad. Ernest Mercier, Executive Vice President and chief of the corporate banking function of Toronto Dominion, tells a typical tale:

> **Fifteen years ago the North American banks had skills and technology ahead of the others. Banking was a sleepy industry abroad. Now there's a more level playing field, and we have to rely on sectoral expertise – foreign exchange, real estate lending, financing the communications sector – these sectors are all international.**

From the experience of the excellent banks, four types of potentially successful strategies for new market penetration emerge.

The first is to build a local business with local skills. Citicorp is the most successful practitioner of this difficult art, although Credit Suisse First Boston has had an outstanding record in the international securities sector. The key challenge is to get the right blend of diversity and central direction. Citicorp's Victor Menezes describes their efforts to build a global meritocracy:

> **We run ourselves as a truly global organization. We tap into the best brain power of the world. About 60 per cent of our international officer staff is non-US. It's a magnificent management training school – the network pays for itself in the quality of the people it sends bubbling up the system.**

Another role model for cross-border expansion via a start-up operation is Credit Suisse's London-based affiliate, Credit Suisse First Boston (CSFB). Since its establishment in the 1970s as a joint venture with a Wall Street house to enter the then-nascent Eurobond market, CSFB has attracted an array of international talent which has not only propelled the firm to the top of most international securities league tables but also created one of the few truly global securities businesses. Its Chairman – and also head of the parent bank international securities business – Hans-Joerg Rudloff – describes how the firm has built its own culture:

You can't export your home culture – it is impossible. Investment banking as known today is an Anglo-Saxon institution; it's not the Continental European or Asian way of doing business. Credit Suisse or other Swiss banks don't have the culture to do Anglo-Saxon style investment banking. Credit Suisse realized it would be wrong to try to impose a change of their very successful way of operating, so they did a joint venture. They were often criticized for choosing that route, but as the last 15 years have shown, they were by far the most successful.

His counterpart at the parent bank – and former chief executive *ad interim* of CSFB – Hans-Ulrich Doerig, a member of the Credit Suisse executive board, agrees:

One of Credit Suisse's strengths is that we have a few important, strong and common denominators plus the flexibility to manage according to our own personality. You have to decentralize; what is successful in Switzerland might not be so in London.

Toronto Dominion's expansion into the US market is another successful form of a *de novo* expansion across borders using local recruits. Chief Executive Officer Dick Thomson describes how it happened:

We got into the US through the US corporate treasurer on Canadian corporate business. The treasurer of a US parent will accept our people on the same basis; we're not looked on as a foreign bank. We've domesticated our US business; we're North American. We let our NY people decide policies; we've accepted that it's a separate tail that can wag the dog.

From the experience of these successful examples of cross border businesses built from scratch, it is clear that the ability to manage diversity is a critical success factor. Another is the ability of a foreign institution to attract outstanding people – clearly the key to Citicorp's success. Bruno Gehrig of Union Bank of Switzerland voices a common view:

A foreign bank has a tougher job to do than its local competitors; you can't succeed with second raters. Mediocrity certainly leads to failures.

A second route to cross border expansion is by acquisition. Given the time frame and bottom line cost over a decade or more to build an indigenous business from scratch, buying such a franchise has an obvious appeal. Among the excellent banks, the HongkongBank stands out as a role model with strategic or controlling stakes taken in James Capel (a leading UK stockbroker), Midland Bank in the UK and Marine Midland in the US. HongkongBank's own culture is that of a federation with considerable delegation to geographic units – a considerable advantage in managing such overseas interests. Peter Brockman, HongkongBank's head of strategic planning and a General Manager, describes the options:

> **When you acquire a company, you acquire its culture. You have two choices: you can destroy the culture, or you can allow it to continue but hopefully educating management to understand your own. It doesn't take place overnight. Arguably we could have been more forceful in encouraging others to be more group-minded.**

One of the recent landmark acquisitions by an excellent bank was the purchase in 1986 by Deutsche Bank of Banca d'America e d'Italia, the Italian retail subsidiary of the Bank of America. Pundits opined about the problems of reconciling the disciplined Deutsche Bank culture with its Italian counterpart – especially as Deutsche has traditionally expanded abroad organically in the past. Yet the anticipated clash has not taken place – in large part because Banca d'America e d'Italia had been well managed by international norms. Hilmar Kopper, a member of Deutsche Bank's management board, makes the point:

> **It would certainly be a mistake to try to turn BAI into a typically German bank – in other words to tear down the BAI sign and replace it with Deutsche Bank's emblem. BAI's potential can be realized only if it retains its identity as an Italian bank. Its management has been left in the hands of Italians.**

National Westminster Bank's acquisition of National Bank of North America is generally regarded as one of the more successful in the US by a European institution. Charles

Green, Deputy Group Chief Executive, describes the results of the bank's approach to expanding by acquisition:

The answer depends on the market. In the US we bought a relatively static bank and used British management to help get it sorted out – and then chose the right management team for its further development.

A third approach to expanding the business base is a true merger in which a common effort is made to bring two or more firms together without a clearly dominant partner. If the straightforward takeovers described above are difficult to carry off, building a totally new culture verges on the impossible. Among all the excellent banks, there is little doubt that S.G. Warburg's four-way merger in anticipation of Big Bang in London is the most exciting case study for the bankologist. Under the leadership of Sir David Scholey of the Warburg merchant bank, three other independent institutions – a stockbroker (Rowe & Pitman), jobber/marketmaker (Ackroyd & Smithers) and gilts dealer (Mullins) were merged to form what, in the view of most London bank-watchers, has become the leading UK full service investment bank. Lord Garmoyle, Vice Chairman of the Group and head of the Warburg corporate finance function, describes their international orientation:

We try to manage on a functional approach global- ly: Tokyo and New York are thus part of the same department. We're the house that is truly internation- al in understanding the international dimension – in acting as a cultural interpreter. Maybe half of our transactions have an international component.

Peter Wilmot Sitwell, another Vice Chairman and the former senior partner of Rowe & Pitman, confirms the difficulty of reorienting a traditional geographic structure:

We've learned a lot. We had geographic reporting; it took us a long time before we realized we had it wrong. Now we have clear functional lines – equities are a function whether it's foreign or domestic.

On a broader scale, the S.G. Warburg merger highlights the difficulty of merging two – much less four – proud,

independent financial institutions. Lord Garmoyle describes
the process:

> **All four firms were strongly led and were preeminent
> in their field. But we all had the same aspirations
> and were comfortable with each other. To get four
> proud organizations to come under one banner, they
> key was to allow all to come forward with ideas rather
> than have a blueprint imposed. There was a common
> approach with all parts of the bank having a say. It
> took a lot of time, a lot of talking with each other, but
> the decisions emerged as a common view.**

On the other side of the Atlantic, interstate banking has
provided the opportunity for geographic expansion by
acquisition – essentially continuing a consolidation process
that took place in the 19th century in most other Western
countries. PNC Financial Corporation and First Wachovia
have been among the major beneficiaries of this trend.

First Wachovia is of particular interest to the student
of bank expansion because of its strong, conservative culture and – at least at the time of writing of *Excellence in
Banking* – apparent lack of interest in the merger process.
John Medlin, First Wachovia's Chief Executive Officer,
explains how the dilemma was resolved:

> **We were comfortable in the context of a single state for
> retail banking, but too small for economies of scale and
> a prominent presence with interstate banking. We could
> have continued on the same path and done well for 5 to
> 10 years, but would have eventually lost ground if we
> didn't expand. We decided to concentrate on one of a
> small number of major metropolitan areas and picked
> Atlanta since it's closer to North Carolina in geography,
> culture, economy and accents. But it was important not
> to do anything to dilute significantly our orientation
> toward quality, soundness, and basic philosphical tenets.**

Chapter 5 will examine the problems encountered in such
mergers in terms of managing different cultures. From the
experience of S.G. Warburg and First Wachovia, however,
it is apparent that the merger strategy involves an extended
time frame, considerable expenditure of senior management

time and possible diversion of effort from the marketplace. Small wonder, then, that excellent banks have often opted for the fourth expansion strategy: one that is product-driven.

A product-driven strategy essentially relies on a real competitive advantage in one or more products to penetrate a non-traditional market – hopefully without a major bricks-and-mortar infrastructure. The trick is to identify such a competitive advantage. It existed for the US money center banks in their penetration of Europe in the 1960s with the new tools of marginal cost lending and loans against cash flows, but since then the vast bulk of new foreign wholesale banking branches throughout the world have relied on traditional loan and deposit products sold on the basis of price, head office relationship or improved service.

In today's market, it is again the US banks who are leading the product assault abroad – this time armed with rate risk management (financial engineering) and leveraged lending products. Bankers Trust is a leading practitioner of the art, and George Vojta, a member of the Management Committee with responsibility for strategic development, explains the virtues of Bankers Trust's leadership in these sectors:

> **If we keep our people positively motivated, we have a natural diversification pattern built into our general franchise. If a product line creates a new market, you can export it. If we can keep doing that successfully, the issue of diversification will take care of itself. We're hesitant to take major positions in vehicles that work according to their own style.**

At excellent US money center banks like Bankers Trust and J.P. Morgan, one hears a lot about 'value added' products – presumably ones which are differentiated from those of the competition. As Bob Engel of Morgan expresses it,

> **We want to be regarded as the premier financial services firm bringing value added products to a limited group of major customers.**

At most of the excellent banking institutions, a product-driven strategy outside a natural customer base means identifying one or more products with a competitive advantage. For the big Swiss banks, the obvious product is global fund management. For Toronto Dominion, it is Canadian dollar foreign exchange. As Bill Brock puts it:

> **Why are we in London and Tokyo today? You can't be in Canadian dollar F/X in isolation. The backbone of our branch in Tokyo is Canadian dollar exchange; our mission in London is the same. They complement our North American strategy. It is one of the few global products we have to offer.**

For First Wachovia, technology-based systems are the cutting edge of a corporate banking strategy outside the Southeastern US. John Medlin explains the choice:

> **Investment banking is foreign to our culture; we can't be unique in that. But we know processing. We'll use technology to eliminate paper and to help build our non-interest income to enhance earnings.**

To sum up the opportunities for expansion outside an existing franchise, the alternatives are clear, but the obstacles are equally formidable. A high level of tolerance of diversity is a prerequisite for successful start-ups abroad as well as acquisitions and mergers. For an organization like a major Swiss, Japanese or British bank built on decades of shared experience and unified by a strong national culture, accepting – much less welcoming – this diversity can be a traumatic experience. One of our panelists puts it graphically:

> **It's a question of intellectual baggage. How do you escape the shackles of local power and prestige to become an innovative, successful challenger abroad?**

In terms of product-driven strategies, not every banking institution can successfully bring together the human and technological skills to develop and sustain a competitive product advantage. Conventional wisdom in the banking world in the late 1980s has it that the pace of product evolution in the highly lucrative sectors such as rate risk management is such that returns on product investment must be recovered in a matter of hours or days before the technology is replicated by the competition. True, but in a host of other sectors – mergers and acquisitions, foreign exchange, leveraged finance, funds management, the lead management of Euro-bonds, etc. – a unique combination of human skills and customer relationships seems to insure leadership positions to the likes of S.G. Warburg, Credit Suisse First Boston and Citicorp, year after year.

The human dimension of these strategies will be discussed subsequently as a success factor; the aspects of managing different cultures will be addressed in Chapter 5.

4 Managing Technology

The user owns the machine; we service it. – Bud McMorran,
Toronto Dominion Bank.

The revolution in information technology for the banking
sector has confronted bank management with an issue which
has vast but uncertain consequences for costs, product
quality and management information. It was foreshadowed
in *Excellence in Banking,* where our focus was on product
innovation. It was then, as now, a central concern of
management in all the excellent banking institutions.

First, a definition of the subject and an analysis of
the problem. What used to be termed electronic data
processing in English (or its equivalent in German,
dataverarbeitung) has been transformed into information
technology (or *informatique* in French). The change in
terminology reflects an equivalent transformation of the use
of the computer from automation of paper flow to reduction
of unit cost; the replacement of manual with computer
processing to today's focus on electronic product delivery
to the retail or corporate customer, the evaluation of client
and product profitability, and analysis of historical price and
yield relationships to develop new risk arbitrage products.

Figure 4.1 portrays the evolution of banking technology
from back room to front office. This transformation has
been a boon to system consultants who are brought in
by a wide array of banks to provide guidance on strategic as well as implementation issues. John Skerritt, a
partner and head of Arthur Andersen's London-based
financial markets group, sums up a standard view of the
issues as seen from the outside:

**Many bankers have placed themselves in the hands of
strangers. Management feels uneasy when confronted
by technicians, and often abdicates; they set the ship off
and hope it arrives. The key issues are that management**

39

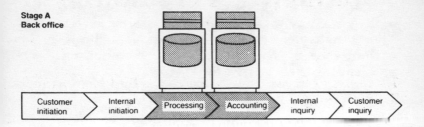

Stage A
Back office

Customer initiation > Internal initiation > Processing > Accounting > Internal inquiry > Customer inquiry

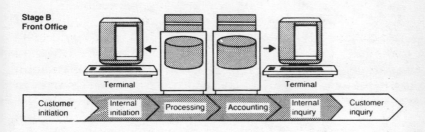

Stage B
Front Office

Terminal · Terminal

Customer initiation > Internal initiation > Processing > Accounting > Internal inquiry > Customer inquiry

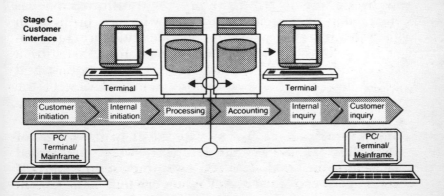

Stage C
Customer interface

Terminal · Terminal

Customer initiation > Internal initiation > Processing > Accounting > Internal inquiry > Customer inquiry

PC/Terminal/Mainframe · PC/Terminal/Mainframe

Figure 4.1

cannot relate spending on technology to business strategy and lack the confidence to treat technology decisions in the same way as other general management decisions. They should not be led by the nose by technicians but challenge every proposal using basic commonsense. The problem for them is that the results of many seemingly innocuous decisions do not emerge for many years, by which time the cost is often staggering and changes to strategy are immensely difficult to achieve.

Simply stated, information technology confounds bank management because:

– the investment cost is staggering – annual investment budgets range between 10 -20% of total operating costs, second in size only to staff costs;

– traditional cost-benefit or other return on investment criteria are increasingly irrelevant as the benefits become more difficult to quantify directly;

– making technology work clearly involves an intimate interaction between technical specialists and senior line management – a goal which is increasingly difficult to achieve;

– there is no assurance that the desired returns will be achieved – or achieved at an acceptable cost. Even the excellent banks have had to go back to the drawing board on individual technology projects.

The need to achieve results through computer technology is thus obvious: better management information, reducing unit costs, new arbitrage products, and direct customer access to the bank's data base to reduce costs and provide better service. Overlaying these virtues, however, is the growing awareness that deregulated banking is increasingly becoming a battleground in which technological superiority will enable a few banks to emerge as the industry's low cost producers. In a sector like banking with minimal product differentiation and deregulation lowering entry barriers, conventional wisdom affirms that being the low cost producer is one of the few possible successful strategies. Even Bankers Trust, an innovative product leader, feels the pressure, as George Vojta points out:

The difference between superior and other competitors will focus on the low cost producer. The edge in relative cost is becoming very powerful. In a freely competitive market, the low cost producer will do best.

At the other end of the product spectrum, John Medlin of First Wachovia agrees:

Our industry has a bloated cost structure. It's difficult when you're doing well to control costs; inflationary growth has us mesmerized. We have to use technology to reduce costs.

Another force driving investment in technology is to shift a bank's human resource balance from processing data to serving the customer. Tom Frost of National Westminster describes the risks and rewards:

The big gamble is technology. Will the customer buy the end product? Do you have it right? – we'll see in two or three years. The issue is delivery; we have to release people. Two thirds of the people in our branch network now deal with systems and one third with clients; our aim is to switch it around.

Management's agony with the technology issue begins with the difficulty – if not impossibility – of measuring the return on a given investment in hardware or software. For managements newly attuned to bottom line profit as a strategic goal, this is doubly frustrating. Yet as investment moves from increasing productivity to improving decision support systems, providing better information or delivering products electronically, so-called strategic, or 'staying in the business', decisions predominate. Each of the excellent banks were asked in the interview process to describe how they measured performance either of a given investment or of the information technology function in general.

The overwhelming response was that every potential performance measure is deeply flawed. Credit Suisse looks at raw data such as the number of people in the data processing function or the cost of hardware but acknowledges that such a measure gives no indication of bottom line effectiveness. Union Bank of Switzerland examines the number of terminals per staff member but admits its limitations. Toronto

Dominion looks at the cost per transaction, but recognizes that it involves subjective allocations of cost.

At Bankers Trust, George Vojta looks at two key ratios on a bank-wide basis: pre-tax income divided by total operating expenses, and revenue return on the appropriate expense base. At the HongkongBank, management uses another pair of bank-wide ratios: technology spending measured as a percentage of total overhead and of the bank's overall profit.

The message is clear: spending today on technology as a whole can be rationalized only at the bank's bottom line, or fairly close to it. Individual ratios may be useful for comparisons over time, but as a decision making tool they are badly flawed. Technological spending is so closely integrated with the bank's core business that tracking individual costs and revenues at an intermediate level is a fool's errand.

At the level of individual investments, a typical response is that of Roger Flemington, Chief Executive of National Westminster's Financial Services sector:

> **We have an internal rate of return for all investment projects which we use as a clear benchmark. We run the rule over it but we also say 'what if we don't do it?'**

Bud McMorran, Executive Vice President and head of Toronto Dominion's information systems function, has a simple answer:

> **You have to talk to the users. I'm fully charged out – they pay for me. There are all sorts of numbers – expenditure levels, lines of code written, cost of transaction – but they don't measure effectiveness. The best way is to go to the users.**

First Wachovia addresses the measurement issue by taking a long term view of relevant costs and revenues. John Medlin analyzes the process:

> **We try to cost all our products. We allocate all costs – it's an art, not a science. We look at the spread between costs and revenues and figure out how we can improve it. What steps can be computerized? What is the break even point of the necessary investment? We don't take a short term view – we go out 5 years or longer.**

If management itself thus finds itself unable to track technology performance except at the bottom line, pity the poor outside analyst attempting to identify the fortunate 'low cost producer' by using publically available data. The cost/revenue and cost/asset ratios which are invariably his only available tools are indeed weak reeds in the face of the problems discussed above plus the inevitable complications posed by different accounting definitions, product mixes and positions on the investment cycle. The outside analyst's classic dilemma remains unresolved; is a high expense ratio a bad thing – does it connote high investment for lucrative future returns or gross inefficiency? Conversely, is a low ratio the product of successful investment in the past or cheeseparing which will have to be corrected by future spending?

There are fortunately more and better answers for the generic problem of how to manage technology as opposed to measuring its performance. The overwhelming response of the excellent banks is for line management to take the lead in managing this central function. Bob Engel of J.P. Morgan sums up his experience:

> **Too often users don't participate in the design stage. We're all guilty of it. Too many senior managers are indifferent and turn it over to a specialist.**

The same view is expressed by another senior line manager, Bruno Gehrig of Union Bank of Switzerland:

> **You need to have technology at the top of the bank; it has to be integrated into the management process. I'm glad we've got two engineers on the Management Board. They have to be involved at the beginning. I chair two major project committees (SOFFEX and ABACUS) and I didn't delegate my responsibilities. If management is a patron you'll have a more efficient use of technology.**

The head of Credit Suisse's technology function, and a member of the Executive Board, Hugo von der Crone, makes the same argument from the specialist's standpoint:

> **The problem is to get the end user to take advantage of the possibilities. Twenty years ago they stopped using the typewriter. You have to bring them back. They only use one tenth of what we can offer them. Top management has to get involved.**

A similar view is expressed by John Littlewood, S.G. Warburg's Director and Head of Administration and Informational Technology, in describing the merger process:

> **There was a tendency for IT to say 'what do you want', and the user to say 'tell me what I can have'. We've realized that both sides are necessary and that you need a continual dialogue and partnership.**

William Purves, the Chairman of Hongkong Bank, expresses the chief executive's point of view:

> **We've got excellent technical strength, but you can't let technology run away with things. We've insisted on providing what the user wanted. Several years ago, we took what they produced. I said – 'unless we can get together, I'll make technical people bankers if the bankers won't get involved'.**

If the core problem is to involve both top management and the users in the technology process, what are the solutions? The first, for most excellent banks, is to move the senior technology officer into the executive suite. The heads of information technology interviewed invariably report directly to the bank's chief executive officer and generally sit on the Management Board or Executive Committee.

The second step is to involve line management in technology. The human obstacles to managing this particular aspect of change are considerable – even in an excellent bank such as First Wachovia. John Medlin describes the problems:

> **Technology needs to be seen in live, day to day applications. Business development people need to see it as a way to offer the customer service – what it does for the customer and the bank. We drip on managers and other people with some of these strategic objectives!**

Even at Citicorp, where technology has been an article of faith for over a decade, progress is slow. Chairman John Reed explains:

> **The problem is our ability to assimilate it. We are hopelessly behind. It is an embarrassment professionally because we know better. My sense is that in five years**

there will be no perceptible improvement in the present situation. In ten years I would hope that Citicorp might take the lead.[1]

Another solution is decentralization of the technology function – once the basic framework is in place as it is in Bankers Trust. The bank's human resource head, Mark Bieler, describes its virtues:

We have a structural bias towards decentralization; systems development groups are spun off to work with businesses. I firmly believe that 75 per cent of the challenge for technologists is the ability to understand the business. It's a self defeating process to design giant systems and apply them to rapidly changing businesses. Small is more beautiful than big in major systems.

Another merit of decentralization is the avoidance of very big mistakes on very expensive big systems. Citicorp's John Reed, a veteran of Citicorp's operations function which he led before becoming Chairman, looks back on an $80 million system under development for two years:

We tried to do too much at once, and it was a tremendous mistake from which I learned a hell of a lot. I'm not sure that I've learned patience yet, but I've since become a fan of getting away from episodic management – big projects – and toward looking for solutions in decent bite sizes.[2]

Another means of getting the ownership of line managers is through techniques such as project committees stacked with users who are actually charged with the technology budget. President of the Executive Board Robert Jeker of Credit Suisse explains their approach:

We're one of the leading banks in technology. The challenge is to solve technical problems and still make money. So you need a project approach. All of our people in technology have to be competitive with outsiders. They're market oriented as a result, and we charge the users. It used to be EDP people who made suggestions; now the line people are.

In thorough Swiss fashion, Credit Suisse implements this project approach with a three-tiered structure designed to involve various levels of line management. As Hugo von der Crone explains:

> **We insure communication at the top with a steering committee headed by a General Manager, to which report working groups composed of users, which approve all projects. Below that there are the individual project groups in charge of specific programs.**

Getting line management to accept allocated technology costs has a remarkable impact on user ownership and responsibility in a profit-driven excellent banking institution. Most of the banks interviewed allocate to user functions at least part of the development and running costs of the new technology. National Westminster, Credit Suisse and Toronto Dominion are among those following this route. As Bud McMorran of Toronto Dominion explains:

> **We're in the banking business using technology, not the other way round. You have to make sure the user has a game plan to execute; are they committed? The great thing is that the user owns the machine; we service it.**

As in any aspect of managing change, communications – between user and technician – is a prerequisite for success. For Union Bank of Switzerland, which has had its share of problems in developing its ABACUS global system, Ekkehard Wildhaber, First Vice President of the bank's information systems department, articulates the problems of getting agreement on a complex project in a multinational structure:

> **We learned a lot in developing systems for the Swiss banking environment. Could we transfer the Swiss experience of ABACUS into the international world? We had to learn again! You need a balance between central control and regional responsibility – the old question of 'knows best vs. knows fastest'. You end up with a rectangle – two sets of line and staff people. The key is that people talk to each other.**

Communication is clearly enhanced by careers which span both the technology function and line jobs – a commitment made by most excellent banks despite the possible short term inefficiencies. Alex Lee, one of HongkongBank's senior Chinese officers and deputy head of the technical services function, describes what happens:

> **It helps to have people who grew up with technology. Both parties have to understand each other – especially as it becomes harder to quantify the benefits of technology. We now spend more time in a more intensive debate. A line manager who started off in EDP can respond more intelligently; it speeds up the process.**

Moving management through the technology function is also an article of faith at Toronto Dominion. Bud McMorran explains:

> **We've taken people from the systems group and moved them out into line jobs. Today you design it, tomorrow you manage a business. It's a big career opportunity, and we've been reasonably successful. It's tougher to do it the other way round. Of the 60 graduates we hire every year for the operations function, some are MBAs who view the systems area as an entry into the bank – we encourage this.**

From a technical standpoint, success is a function of developing the appropriate architecture within which systems for individual products, which are evolving continually in sectors such as rate risk management, can be developed on a decentralized basis. Bankers Trust is one of the few which have reached this systems Nirvana, and George Vojta describes how it works:

> **It all has to be controlled by an architecture – a workable blueprint for systems applications for the whole company. It usually doesn't exist: most banks have competing systems and lots of duplication of expense. It's tough to get out of this problem; you may have to write off these costs. We have the architecture – that's the key.**

Such a diversity of systems exists in many of the excellent banks – usually in view of the overwhelming cost of totally revamping the existing incompatible systems.

Ekkehard Wildhaber of Union Bank of Switzerland sums up such a dilemma:

> **We have to migrate over time. Our acquisitions have their own hardware and systems. We'll continue to have lots of different hardware, even in Zurich. We have to live with it.**

Another dimension of managing technology is the factor of time – of critical importance to anxious line managers competing for scarce resources and driven by market needs. John Littlewood of S.G. Warburg describes the challenge faced by management confronted with four different systems at the time of the merger:

> **It took lots of time. Two and a half years [before Big Bang] was barely enough time to get the IT side right. Preparing for Big Bang was a race against time, but we arrived on time. We successfully met the challenge of merging the IT systems of four different firms.**

Another lesson being learned by the excellent banks is that technology development is a never ending saga. New product innovation, improving hardware and software and expanding into new markets means that IT spending goes on and on. As Tom Frost of National Westminster puts it:

> **It never ends – it's like the sea. The opportunities are ever-rolling – we're on a moving roller coaster.**

Several excellent banks aim at a balance between being a pioneer and a laggard in technology. John Medlin of First Wachovia puts the case:

> **It is important not to be left behind, but also not to be too far out front. The objective is to be the low cost provider of high quality service, which is a goal seldom achieved by the laggard or the trailblazer. You want to be near the leading edge, but you want to avoid being on the 'bleeding' edge.**

A necessary footnote to the agreed need to upgrade technology in a bank's structure is to ensure that the specialists themselves are up to speed. Whereas the trend – as indicated by Bankers Trust's experience – is to move technology out into the product functions, Credit Suisse found that it was unable to attract and retain superior technical specialists in the 1970s. The solution was to create a new culture in the systems function – in part by centralizing the entire back office function in the Zurich region into a separate facility in the suburb of Uetlihof. As Harry Huerziler of Credit Suisse's operations function puts it:

> **We wanted a more equal partnership between line and operations. The front office would take the best people; the operations got the rest. We were the underdogs until we got our own building in 1980. Top management realized that they had to do something to raise the quality to that of the other divisions, so we centralized the back office. We needed a different culture in the back office: the work is different; you have people with different motivations. There have been enormous productivity increases.**

To sum up, the technology issue can be regarded as a classic laboratory test of managing change. The solutions are straightforward: getting top management to focus on the problem, improve communication, give line managers a taste of technological responsibility, adopt a project management approach and develop the appropriate central architecture. Yet the vast financial stakes involved and the human resistance to change raise the issue to the top of many excellent banks' problem list. Looking at the high degree of correlation between the age of the line managers and resistance to change, one is tempted to agree with Bud McMorran of Toronto Dominion when he says that:

> **This is a generational thing.**

5 Managing Different Cultures

We can't just buy someone and hope he'll understand our culture. – Robert Jeker, Credit Suisse.

One of the themes of *Excellence in Banking* was the strength provided by shared values in dealing with a variety of management challenges. Managements were quick to focus on the virtues of a single culture which facilitated communication, created a sense of identity and focussed on strategic priorities. But a minority view acknowledged that market challenges would force management to deal with more than one culture. That minority view has now become received wisdom. Moving into diverse businesses, buying into overseas markets and recruiting outside specialists for key functional tasks has persuaded even the excellent banks with the strongest unitary system of shared values that something has to change. The focus of this chapter is how the excellent banks are dealing with this challenge.

Perhaps the most shattering experience has come in the securities sector as banks – even the European universal institutions with their domestic securities experience – come to grips with the challenge of motivating and controlling highly incentivized and motivated product specialists without destroying the morale of the rest of the business. The Big Bang in London and elsewhere has had its explosive impact on corporate culture as well as banks' product offerings.

Credit Suisse, with its strong universal banking tradition and ownership of the leading international securities business, is a useful guinea pig for this cultural experiment. Hans-Ulrich Doerig expounds the virtues of decentralization:

It's a mistake to impose your own culture. The solution is to expose your people to different cultures. It starts at the top. We send people outside to work in different

cultures to get an understanding of people in the field. There's an increasing meshing of cultures on a global scale – a softening of cultural differences.

Cultural diversity has always been a hallmark of Citicorp's ethos, but the bank's product and geographic thrust has created a new dimension, as Pam Flaherty, Citicorp's Senior Human Resources Officer, explains:

> **We're more comfortable than most with managing vast multinational operations, but it's still a challenge. With our heavy component of retail, our people do lots of very different things; we have more specialists than ever before. As an example, we might have people who are the world's best in credit card solicitation by mail; they know everything about Zip codes in the US and really know how to go about mail solicitation. We're skewing towards the specialist. The challenge is to develop leaders from this narrow experience base. We bring in outsiders on the assumption they will be key members of Citicorp; they came because they want to be part of the team. The question is: Are we willing to make the investment in helping them do more things?**

For most excellent banks, the issue is diversity between home country and foreign culture – effectively one of the dimensions of geographic expansion addressed in Chapter 3. For others, it is the successful meshing of traditional commercial banking with an investment banking function acquired or built internally. While some excellent banks have grown their own securities business to eliminate or minimize the cultural conflict, success is only relative. J. P. Morgan has been one of the most articulate of the excellent institutions in fostering the home grown variety, but as Bob Engel points out, the path has not been trouble free:

> **There are two cultures, and the process has to be managed. There are two different avenues people choose, stemming from entirely different sets of ground rules by which clients do business.**

The management challenge is thus obvious: to achieve a sense of common purpose, a common ground, which blends the different cultures yet allows each to function effectively in the marketplace and the internal dialogue.

Having acknowledged that diversity is here to stay, the excellent banks also agree – at least in theory – that the solution is not to destroy the existing value systems. As the comments in Chapter 3 affirm, banks like HongkongBank, Credit Suisse, National Westminster and Deutsche Bank are committed to retaining local values. The blending argument is particularly relevant when a core business is involved – especially when one is selling different products to the same client. Terry Green, Deputy Group Chief Executive and the National Westminster officer given responsibility for the investment banking subsidiary NatWest Investment Bank, believes that:

> **If it really is an integrated business because the customer demands it, you have to integrate. Lombard North Central [in consumer finance] kept its own culture; it doesn't have a common customer base. It's a question of being part of the core strategy; if there aren't the synergies, you don't have to run it like the other businesses.**

The same view of a core business is expressed at Bankers Trust. Joe Manganello points out that:

> **We had a lively debate about how to sell different products to the same customer. There has to be some coordination. When you throw 11 product managers at one client, he asks 'who's in charge?' In this business, you sell the institution as well as the product.**

The challenge of establishing a common purpose is aggravated by the massive infusion of specialists, which not only creates greater diversity but makes it more difficult to implement the excellent bank's preference for moving people around to create the basis for common understanding. Citicorp's Pam Flaherty articulates the dilemma:

> **There's a tradition here of embracing and accepting two kinds of people: long term career types and professionals hired in from the market. I think that's a healthy trend and one that will continue.**

Once again, the challenge is clear. What are the excellent banks doing to meet it? The first solution is to create –

or reinforce – core common values which are relevant regardless of job description. S.G. Warburg, J.P. Morgan, First Wachovia and Bankers Trust each have their own set of core values. First, listen to Lord Garmoyle of S.G. Warburg:

> **We maintain the ethos of giving disinterested advice. All [of the component firms] are convinced of the rightness of this approach. We've deemphasized the star approach and encouraged people to share their decisions.**

At First Wachovia, preserving the key tenets of the Wachovia culture was a cornerstone of the merger process with First Atlanta. John Medlin explains:

> **It's important to go back to basics; it should be the first subject for any merger discussion. You can't do five mergers at once – you'll dilute the standard of quality. It was important not to do anything to dilute significantly our orientation toward the basic principles of quality and soundness – our basic philosophical tenets.**

For J.P. Morgan, Jack Morgan's tenet of doing first class business in a first class way has been joined by the concept of adding value. As Bob Engel puts it:

> **We're still in the basic business of bringing added value to our client base. People want us for our brains. The challenge is to do it in an entrepreneurial environment.**

Unlike its Canadian peers, Toronto Dominion has eschewed the acquisition route into investment banking to preserve its value system. As Dick Thomson puts it:

> **We're turning corporate bankers into securities people. We're going to make it one culture. We've decided to be excellent in each business we enter.**

The issue of incentive compensation is raised early in most conversations with the excellent banks on the topic of managing different cultures. Urban Joseph, Toronto Dominion's head of human resources, describes the central role played by this issue in an organization which, at the time of writing *Excellence in Banking*, was committed to a bank-wide bonus system with little financial recognition of individual effort:

You need all the dimensions of human resource management: recruitment, training, organizational development, compensation and employee relations. If you miss on one cylinder, you're not performing well. But the lynchpin – and the toughest to execute – is hard performance appraisal and a counselling culture.

From this and other conversations with excellent banks, it was clear that the lynchpin – in the sense of the pressure point – of conflicting cultures is the compensation structure, particularly in an investment banking environment where incentive compensation is a substantial portion of the whole. By the same token, incentive compensation is widely used to reinforce the banking institution's shared values.

At Bankers Trust, for example, which is totally committed to rewarding individual performance, Mark Bieler outlines the role incentive compensation plays:

People are very attentive to discords between our strategy and our execution. We spend a lot of time listening for these discords. For example, if a selfish group interested only in their own bottom line is overly rewarded, you have created a mixed message. That's why, when our Management Committee reviews bonuses, it asks: 'Are they collaborative?' and then shapes bonuses accordingly. The alternative of creating fee splitting would become a national pastime and would create a similar mixed message.

The compensation structure plays the same cultural role in bringing together investment and commercial bankers at Toronto Dominion. Urban Joseph describes a recently-introduced scheme:

How do you manage traditional commercial banking and investment banking and still retain the strength of both without civil war? The solution is through compensation. It's the glue that holds it together or can blow it apart. There's a perceived difference in contribution; the trick is for all to feel valuable. You can lose out if you're not a team player. No one person can deliver the deal in our business. Top management makes the decision as a group.

The same message of common purpose is given in S.G. Warburg's compensation structure, which was built on totally disparate programs for commercial bankers, stockbrokers and traders. Hugh Stevenson explains how it works:

> **We needed time to get it right. We had the complete range, but when you added them up, it was mainly a question of shuffling the cards with a different mix. Sometimes it felt like riding a bike on the tightrope and not falling off. You can't be totally fair in this business. But we are all in it together; that helps.**

Yet the genie has been let out of the bottle. The conflicts raised by variable compensation cause some anguish at banks like Citicorp. As George Davis puts it:

> **There's a challenge to high paying jobs in terms of the historical culture. Clearly, at Citicorp there are different packages for different types of work. We don't know quite how to handle it yet except to say that we are learning as we go.**

Perhaps the most straightforward solution to the problem of dual cultures is to grow one's own to minimize, if not eliminate, the cultural gap. This is the preferred solution of J.P. Morgan, Toronto Dominion, First Wachovia and others. These excellent banks affirm that their solution is more time consuming but, in the long term, offers a more solid achievement in view of the energy required to assimilate the culture of an acquired entity. Ernest Mercier explains why Toronto Dominion grew its own investment bankers rather than follow the acquisition route of its peers:

> **We have the customer list; what we need is brainpower. The issue is how to retrain and develop people. Everyone has the sense of being in at the ground floor. There's a very positive feeling; we know we're going to get there, and it's fun to be part of it. There's not a we/they situation as in the case of an acquisition with a tremendous pressure to perform.**

Yet growing one's own investment bankers cannot eliminate the divisive influence of incentive compensation and different skills base which separate relationship managers from product specialists. Of all the excellent banks, J.P. Morgan has prided itself in training its own investment bankers in the Morgan culture, yet as Bob Engel points out,

> **There's a fine balance between relationship and transaction. The requirements of the latter are so complicated that the old-line guy just can't get by. You can't expect relationship managers to be all things to all people.**

A fascinating perspective on the 'make vs. buy' decision on building an investment banking capability is that of National Westminster Bank, which has relied heavily on acquisitions and outside recruitment to build its County NatWest unit. Terry Green, a career NatWest banker who took over responsibility for the investment banking unit after the departure of the original executives heading the business, sums up his views:

> **There were a lot of different cultures – stock brokerage, research, trading and so forth. Those individual cultures were overwhelmed when they moved into a large, expanding organization. We did not ensure that sufficient cultural values were established which would not only relate to the rest of NatWest but would also enable these growing activities to thrive.**

One of the other excellent bankers, in analyzing NatWest's investment banking prospects, agrees:

> **They'll have to build a culture from scratch; it's much more difficult. They should build it around a series of individuals with the necessary authority and charisma – but also in sync with the parent organisation.**

The healing process of time also enables natural leadership to emerge and provide the glue to unite different cultures. The HongkongBank's federalist culture has shaped its approach to the securities businesses it has acquired, as Peter Brockman points out:

> **The capital markets area has been a very difficult one for us to handle. It made no sense to build one global capital market business; the units would have lost their own sense of identity. Instead we're moving toward a**

situation in which the business areas have developed
recognized leaders, or flagships. We don't rule out overlaps. All the players have come to know each other over
the years; it's taken time, but there's more cohesion.

In their thrust into the investment banking business,
the excellent commercial banks have borrowed from their
Wall Street competitors the concept of partnership. This
is expressed most often in terms of the 'buy side-sell side'
relationship: the need of originators, working with clients,
to collaborate with traders and salesmen who are in touch
with the marketplace. Charles Baillie, head of Toronto
Dominion's 'sell', or investment banking side, puts it neatly:

> We make sure that we can't live without the relationship
> managers. There's an effort to convince everyone that
> investment banking isn't the glamorous job. It's a team
> approach. There are the same financial incentives for
> both groups. Why would you refer a deal to a guy
> who's getting a lot more from a deal than you? We
> sit down at bonus time and comment on each other's
> people's contribution – our people know that.

The word 'partnership' is heard more often as well in
the corridors of Citicorp, an institution which in the past
has fostered internal competition to achieve excellence. As
George Davis, who runs a major 'buy side' or relationship
management function for Citicorp explains:

> The tension has gone; people are working together
> well. A partnership is like a marriage; you have to
> work at it. I don't know a better way to put it.

Another bank which has realized the limits of internal competition between cultures is Bankers Trust. Joe Manganello
describes one of the lessons learned in the decade during
which the bank built its investment banking business:

> We brought in lots of new talent to do the new business,
> but we found that we had lots of quality, adaptable
> talent already here. Some of the dogs weren't too old;
> they just needed a ringmaster willing to have them
> perform. The old credit skills enabled us to do leveraged
> finance, for example, which led to M and A and private

placements. The two cultures have to be melded, not managed separately.

Another classical solution to the problem of different cultures is strong communication and shared decision making. Chairman David Scholey of S.G. Warburg attributes the success of Warburg's unique four-way merger to shared decision making from the outset:

> **We brought together people from the four component firms so there was a great deal of familiarization and cross fertilization at an early stage. This established by general recognition who were the most experienced figures in each case to lead a function.[1]**

His colleague Peter Wilmot Sitwell agrees that the well-known Warburg bias towards overpowering internal communication worked well in the merger context:

> **We formed a steering group from all four firms which met weekly for 18 months. The secret is to keep that balance – to allow the smaller components to feel they have just as much to say as anybody else. There were endless get-togethers. It was not 'I'm God – I own you'.**

J.P. Morgan is another advocate of strong internal communications. Bruce Brackenridge, Morgan's head of administration and Group Executive, argues that one of management's principal challenges in bridging the commercial and investment banking cultures is a new form of communication:

> **Within the overall business of managing change what is critical is learning how to communicate in a flat organization. You need a different mindset to get people to communicate laterally – to figure out what other people laterally in the organization might want from your new product. Your networking has to be a lot more horizontal as opposed to the vertical communication of a commercial bank.**

The final word from the ranks of the excellent banks in dealing with different cultures is to retain the central elements of one's own culture. While the excellent German and Swiss banks are outspoken in their commitment not to impose their own culture on overseas units, there is an equally strong determination that core home country values be acknowledged. Robert Jeker of Credit Suisse discusses the issue in the context of CSFB's different culture:

We're used to the problem of managing different cultures. We know it's a problem! We can't just buy someone and hope he'll understand our culture. Our structure allows different cultures with some important parts in common – profitability, quality and our three core values of competence, speed and friendliness.

In the process of assimilating different cultures, Deutsche Bank lags behind many of its excellent peers. Ellen Schneider-Lenné, a deputy member of the Vorstand, regards this as the bank's principal challenge:

We need to become a more multinational bank. How well can we integrate local people with their strengths into Deutsche Bank? Now that we're taking in people from the outside, how do you make them fit in without losing what made them attractive in the first place?

In the efforts by National Westminster Bank to restructure and redirect its investment banking subsidiary, one senses the same concern about core values. As Charles Green puts it:

We had to learn some things the hard way. There was a lot of pressure to get started in investment banking, which led to some unfortunate cultural problems which have taken time to work through. We should perhaps have followed our instincts and the NatWest tradition that's served us well through many changes of circumstances, and what in fact has kept us alive.

To summarize the issue of managing different cultures, the guidelines established by the excellent banks are clear: patience, the reinforcement of common core values, good communication, the effective use of compensation to reinforce cultural values, and growing one's own to the extent possible.

Yet the experience of the excellent banks indicates that the way forward for most will be long and arduous. Union Bank of Switzerland is embarking on a program of regional decentralization which will also involve integrating formerly autonomous units such as stockbroker Phillips and Drew. Mathis Cabiallavetta, who as Executive Vice President has responsibility for overseas units, takes the long term view:

> **Despite some initial problems, I would not overestimate the issue of integration in the longer term. The integration of cultures will lead to a more flexible and more professional bank.**

Rudi Mueller, UBS' Executive Vice President with responsibility for all the bank's UK businesses, describes his experience in blending the British stockbrokerage culture of Phillips and Drew and UBS' shared values:

> **Phillips and Drew developed out of a partnership with a totally flat structure. The Board was like an arbitration council with most decisions coming up to them, in contrast to UBS where we have clearer delegation down the line and where a manager knows what his responsibility is. We're working hard to change the old culture. It's more difficult than we anticipated. We're trying to classify jobs by responsibilities, abilities and functions. But we have the advantage of a very good stock of young British people with above-average education. It is our objective to explain and inform UBS policy to them and to future employees. We're not just bringing in an army of Swiss executives – we don't have them available and we don't need them.**

In an entirely different business, that of merging two US regional banks, one senses from talking with the management of First Wachovia that bringing together even two like-minded banks has been less easy than contemplated. John Medlin summarizes the process:

> **There was the culture of a large urban area [Atlanta] and one that was widely dispersed [Wachovia]. You need to drop back and look at the human factors. It's a balance between tolerance and impatience. First someone has to explain how to do things, then the others have to believe in it and demonstrate the ability to practice it. But it takes time and trial and error.**

His colleagues describe in more detail how detailed credit and management accounting procedures had to be implemented in the merged bank. Jack Runnion, First Wachovia's chief financial officer and Executive Vice President, sums it up:

> **Things look a lot simpler than they are. You couldn't tell people from the two banks apart in a social gathering. But in reality the management systems were very different – like a single wing and a T formation offense in football. It initially caused a lot of trauma. One management style will prevail: you can't mix and match different approaches to management.**

A final – and negative – comment comes from one of our panelists:

> **Within banks in general there's a high degree of arteriosclerosis – of bureaucracy. There's a low tolerance for dissent, and inadequate tolerance for diversity.**

6 Strategy: Competitive Advantage in an Uncertain World

You need a certain degree of contrariness – of disciplined entrepreneurship. – John Medlin, First Wachovia.

A chapter in *Excellence in Banking* on strategic planning concluded – perhaps surprisingly - that such planning did not rank very high on the agendas of the excellent institutions. Virtually all had a strong sense of who they were and where they were going. Planning for some was therefore delegated to operating units; for others it took the form of one-off scenario analysis or an extended budgeting process – hardly an exercise in strategic positioning.

Four years later, times have changed – perhaps the most significant transformation revealed in the interviews. The winds of change have indeed ruffled the waters throughout the banking world. Even the US money center banks which had knowingly embarked on a perilous course towards global investment banking exhibit a level of heightened anxiety – as do their excellent counterparts in Europe and the Far East. When asked to articulate the issues of most concern to them, banker after banker prefaced his response with a litany of environmental pressures which had emerged since the interviews in 1984.

Concern over strategic direction focuses first on getting priorities right in an overcrowded market. The question of 'what business are we in' preoccupies particularly the US money center banks. George Davis of Citicorp puts it vividly:

Our problem is identical to the other major US banks; we're no longer bankers – we're financial intermediaries of some sort. We know we're not in the same business we were five years ago, but we're not sure what we'll be in

the future. Our product line has changed; 50 per cent of my business today is deals; I have a potentially highly variable income stream. The art form has changed; in terms of actual deal doing, I'm technologically obsolete considering what I was trained for.

The uncertainty is echoed at J.P. Morgan. Chairman Lew Preston explains the new approach:

The external pressures, the speed of change in technology and information, mean that senior people have got to do more strategic thinking and not be locked into the old strategic plan that you dust off once a year.[1]

Bob Engel, a member of the Chairman's Office who was taken from a senior line job to focus exclusively on strategic planning, describes his new task:

I'm looking at our business in the context of longer term opportunities outside of the present parameters. Should we go retail? What business are we really in?

One of his colleagues at Morgan describes the dilemma:

The issue is to build new profitable revenue streams. In the past, people shared assumptions about where we were going. It was like being on automatic pilot — such a strong implied understanding of the marching orders. Now we have to figure out what the orders are — we need a process, a forum, a mechanism to set priorities and allocate resources.

Across the Atlantic and north of the Canadian border, the issue is one of choice, of allocating limited resources. For the excellent European banks with powerful national franchises yet the human and financial resources to play a role beyond national borders, the choice involves language such as 'global player', 'multinational bank', 'regional institution' and the like. Even Deutsche Bank, with its expressed commitment to play on the global investment banking stage, has its doubts, as chief financial officer and Deputy Vorstand member Juergen Krumnow points out:

The issue is to find the right strategy. It's a question of self-understanding. A lot of people think that we should

be a German bank with some international offices and that we should grow our present 6 per cent German market share to, say, 10 per cent. Others say 'We should go global and be in the top 20 worldwide'. We can't do both – our management resources are limited.

The same sense of limitation preoccupies another powerful, well-capitalized bank with global reach – Hongkong Bank. Chief planning officer Peter Brockman refers to the imposition of global capital adequacy ratios:

The capital constraint hasn't been a source of worry in the past – now it is. In this volatile world there's no Big Daddy to help us out.

At Toronto Dominion, which boasts a highly successful domestic franchise plus a sophisticated corporate lending business in the US, Bill Brock articulates the choices for a strong North American regional bank:

What do you do outside your borders? Should we widen our North American base – if so, can you do it without an acquisition? Our Canadian business is mature, but can we afford the technology to be in all segments of the Canadian market and still be competitive abroad? Toronto Dominion is a superregional with a second leg of global corporates. You can't be second class in either business or you're dead.

The issue of resource allocation is heightened by a growing awareness of vulnerability of cost structures – in both the retail and corporate businesses. The preoccupation with steadily rising costs against a backdrop of revenues which are both volatile and compressed by competition thus permeates the thinking of all the excellent banks. A familiar refrain is heard from Deutsche Bank's Juergen Krumnow:

In retail we need to be the low cost producer. We'll segment the market, go towards the high net worth individual, and split up the branches. It's tough, but we have to reduce costs.

The same point is made at another major retail institution, Toronto Dominion. Dick Thomson lists being a low cost producer as a critical success factor:

This is a low margin business. If your competition forces you to double your opening hours, there are big cost implications; there'll be some winners and losers.

Relative efficiency is also a critical success factor for Bankers Trust at the other end of the product spectrum. George Vojta expresses a common view:

In a deregulated market, it's hard to get a permanent niche, so that the difference between a superior player and the others will focus on being the low cost producer. The edge in relative cost is becoming very powerful.

The juxtaposition of concern for costs and uncertainty over expansion priorities leads to a host of issues. Can one afford to be in both the retail and wholesale businesses? Bankers Trust's bold decision in the 1970s to drop the former is very much in the minds of its peers. How attractive is lending money in any market segment? Executives at First Wachovia contemplate the relative attractions of the banking business as against their highly profitable specialty of data processing. And expansion via acquisition or grass roots development in new market areas is a choice of universal interest.

So what are the answers to these dilemmas? Have the excellènt banks any particular solutions for their banking brethren?

The first response is the consultant's textbook solution: build on one's strengths. In the merchant banking business, Lord Garmoyle of S.G. Warburg summarizes the group's approach:

I'm not sure we've been strategists, but we add to things we do well; if we do badly, we deemphasize it. It's a gradualist approach – not giant conceptual steps.

For Charlie Sanford, Chief Executive Officer of Bankers Trust, the key word is 'focus':

We want to be among the top 10 financial institutions in the world. To be in the top 10 every one will have to be a niche player. If we continue to get the right people and maintain our focus, we'll get there. Ours is not a business where conglomerates can work.[2]

A specific strategy in the investment banking sector which builds on natural strengths is that of Toronto Dominion in marketing fixed interest securities through its domestic branch network. Whereas its peers in Canada, the UK and Australia have followed the more traditional route of acquiring a professional sales and trading capability in the securities sector, Toronto Dominion has built on its natural placing power, as Charles Baillie explains:

> **We picked areas where we had a relative advantage: discount brokerage, money market paper, M and A, mutual funds, bond underwriting, corporate advisory services. Our relative strength is our branches; if we don't use them they'll be albatrosses. We don't worry about cannibalizing our deposit base; the volume of third party money market paper is actually greater than personal savings deposits.**

Among the US superregional commercial banks, PNC has built its competitive strategy on extending product reach over a broader client base through acquisitions. Charles Thayer, PNC's Executive Vice President, explains:

> **The primary focus is revenue enhancement; there are usually insufficient economics of scale to justify an acquisition. We've developed competitive services – cash management, private placements, credit card processing, student loans, discount brokerage, processing money market mutual funds, and investment research. Through the acquisition process, banks in Kentucky and Ohio can thus get absolutely state of the art technology and thus more business with existing customers as well as customers of competitors across the street. If the Glass Steagall law restricting investment banking activities is changed, we'll be able to offer a turn-key capability in investment research and mutual fund operations to other financial institutions.**

For Citicorp, strength in credit assessment is the key building block. George Davis elaborates:

> **Our competitive strength is credit. We're technically good and do best in complex credit situations. We've**

brought leveraged lending to Europe. I don't care about being in the UK gilts market – I prefer to have a competitive advantage.

Bob Engel of J.P. Morgan sums it up:

The most important success factor is to identify our strengths and build on them. We don't try to dance with all the girls on the street.

'Not dancing with all the girls on the street' flies in the face of another theme of conventional banking wisdom – that of offering a full line of banking services. Yet competitive pressures are forcing banks in one market after another to pick and choose, to focus on a more limited product range and leave others to the competition.

The second lesson from the excellent banks is realism: a strategy which reflects competitive reality rather than the triumph of hope over experience. Mark Bieler of Bankers Trust lists this as his most important success factor:

You have to be scrupulously honest with yourself about what you add. Copycats will lose. Getting out of retail was big news; we did it because we weren't likely to be number one or two. It requires a special kind of leadership. Charlie [Sanford] is a visionary; he's also intellectually honest – painfully so with us.

This honesty has earned the admiration of Bankers Trust's excellent peers; a senior officer of one of the excellent European banks struggling with its own strategy acknowledges it:

Bankers Trust burned the boats: what courage! I'm full of admiration. We go step by step; we'll always walk; I doubt we'll jump.

Another excellent bank that prides itself on honesty – derived from constant internal challenging of assumptions – is Citicorp. The bottom-up form of intellectual honesty is described by Victor Menezes:

The worst thing that can happen to an organization is that all wisdom emanates from head office.

Another dimension of realism is to open the organizational windows to let in the external environment –

a problem for many banks embroiled in analyzing their strengths and weaknesses. Victor Menezes continues:

> **We need to bring a sense of external reality into Citicorp. We can get awfully inbred here; there's a risk of saying 'We're doing great but the market doesn't understand us.'**

Probably the greatest gap between external reality and individual bank strategy at the time of writing this book is that between the 40-odd aspirants in the global securities business – including most of the excellent banks – and the 10-15 which in the late 1980s were universally acknowledged to be able to play a profitable role in this prestigious but intensely competitive market. George Vojta of Bankers Trust makes the point – without putting names to the winners and losers:

> **There are 35-40 global competitors, of which maybe 10-15 will establish a long run competitive position. What does it take? – size, earning power, a tradition of globalism, adequate legal powers, technology, relative efficiency and the quality of people.**

A third recommendation from the excellent banks is to take the big bet – and, of course, to get it right. First Wachovia's move into data processing on a national scale, Citicorp's decision in 1979 to move aggressively into consumer banking, Bankers Trust's sale of its retail business, HongkongBank's bold strategic acquisitions, and S.G. Warburg's opportunistic approach to the Big Bang in London – all belie the caution which the excellent banks generally apply to investments in technology, risk management and most other day-to-day decisions.

Listen first to Warburg's Hugh Stevenson:

> **What lessons have we learned? First, that our success is due to thinking out at an early stage where we wanted to be. We're a postwar creation; it has always been a struggle – we take nothing for granted. Big Bang was a big opportunity for us to do things we hadn't been able to do – it opened up the gilts and equities markets.**

Citicorp is another believer in the big, bold decision. Head planner Victor Menezes puts it in graphic terms:

The biggest issue is how to buck the conventional mold. It pervades our industry; we move in lemming-like fashion across the world. Conventional wisdom is almost always wrong; it tends to diminish spreads and increase risk. Walter Wriston bet on retail banking; it was successful – by itself, Citicorp's consumer bank would be the second largest bank in the US and it did not exist 10 years ago. A question to ponder: where will the next wave come from?

Perhaps most surprising of all is the strength of the contrarian spirit at First Wachovia, an institution which prides itself on survival and rigorous focus on risk. John Medlin explains what he considers the first success factor in banking:

You need a certain degree of contrariness. If you're doing the same thing everyone else is, you'll only be average. You have to be a little earlier or better – or avoid the popular things. When the market is a shambles, you have to go out and take risks. The time to make sporty loans is when times are tough. It's disciplined entrepreneurship.

This theme of entrepreneurship in the strategic dimension is echoed by other excellent banks. Dick Thomson describes his approach at Toronto Dominion:

We preach 'think change'. We don't think of a five year plan. Every day is different; no policy lasts more than a day. Policies are a way to go to sleep.

The opportunistic approach is alive and well at Citicorp. George Davis offers his view:

Citicorp's corporate finance area is very opportunistic. Going forward, we'll have to make some strategic decisions. Given the rapid evolution in the market, you can still be opportunistic, but you need a clear view of the future.

In sum, the pressures of an unfriendly environment in the late 1980s have forced the excellent banks – both those like Citicorp who are instinctively opportunistic and those like J.P. Morgan and Deutsche Bank which have long marched to a traditional tune – to reexamine their priorities and competitive positioning.

The bankologist's first conclusion is that many excellent banks still have a long way to travel. Deutsche Bank's struggle to establish priorities reflects in many respects the reverse side of being number one, as Ulrich Weiss, a member of the Vorstand and head of human resources, puts it:

> **Our big task is not to be burdened by success in facing past challenges. It's more difficult for a successful bank to sense the need for change if you have a problem. The time has come when we have to change faster. It's comparable to the period between 1870 and 1914 – a period of innovative thrust for the bank.**

Having made the big decisions on strategic direction, the challenge then is to stick with a strategy when market conditions – read 'competition' – make life uncomfortable. Bankers Trust is such an excellent bank which has been bold, consistent, and highly successful. Yet Joe Manganello bemoans its vulnerability to others which in logic should not be on the same playing field:

> **We can demonstrate value added. What bothers us the most is what to do about the 'cheap and dumb' institutions – those who are easy on credit standards and trying to buy business by not charging enough.**

The profusion of aggressive competitors in the global securities business is particularly aggravating to an industry leader like Credit Suisse First Boston. CSFB's Hans-Joerg Rudloff deplores the relative absence of strategic thinking:

> **We're in a huge structural crisis; the entire financial industry will restructure. No one has any idea of where they are going. Many are headless chickens with no intellectual grip on the fast changes. Management has no time to think – to reflect – they're just travelling around. Investment banking gets carried along on the wave. Managements don't have the guts to go against the Street so they ride a wave to disaster.**

Finally, getting the balance right between flexibility and direction is not an easy task for the best of the excellent banks. For J.P. Morgan's Bob Engel,

> **One of the critical issues is to make sure you continue to have an entrepreneurial environment. It's the balance between flexibility and critical mass; you need to give the innovators an opportunity to breathe.**

In the same vein, Toronto Dominion's Dick Thomson cautions his colleagues that policies – including strategies – are sleep-inducing. Yet the outside observer is fascinated by the trade-off at banks like Citicorp between internal friction and a clear strategy; is there, he wonders, an inevitable loss of entrepreneurial drive when strategic direction – however enlightened – is put in place?

7 Critical Mass: The Reality Behind the Conventional Wisdom

Every business has a critical mass. – Dick Thomson, Toronto Dominion.

Management consultancy is a jargon-filled business. Amidst this jargon, however, are a few nuggets, and one of them is the phrase 'critical success factor'. Asking a businessman what separates the sheep from the goats in his business often has a remarkable impact in focussing in on a limited number of distinguishing characteristics and wiping away the jargon that inevitably is used to mystify the outsider.

Armed with this weapon, the author asked most of the excellent bankers what they regarded as the critical success factors in the banking business. The responses form the core of Chapters 7-10. Remarkably enough, this question elicited more thoughtful and detailed answers than the initial one on critical issues – an indication perhaps of the banker's interest in a period of rapid change of reducing a broad array of variables to a few simple but relevant truths.

The first key success factor – and the subject of this chapter – is critical mass. This phrase itself reeks of jargon and was initially put forward in the interviews as a straw man – a question to demonstrate the irrelevance of size in banking. But as bankers responded and articulated the reality of physical size, it became quite clear that some form of such measurement was indeed a critical success factor in banking.

Even the most casual observer of the banking scene is struck by bankers' concern with relative size. Perhaps initially a product of a regulated era when prestige and earning power correlated with physical presence and market share, it continues with an intense preoccupation for most bankers on league tables – which, in most cases, continue to rank banks on asset size. Notwithstanding the multitude of factors – securitization, capital adequacy rules and the like – which have come to disassociate earning power from balance sheet size, both bankers and analysts around the world still in large part rank banks on the latter rather than former criterion.

The thrust of the questioning in the interviews was thus designed to probe beyond the ego and image-dominated aspect of size and determine how, in a ferociously competitive world, size actually matters. What is critical mass? In a world which is presumably capital short, but which is sufficiently competitive to reduce the return on incremental capital, how important is it in reality to have a larger capital base than a rival? And is there any magical figure – a threshold – beyond which a bank is truly in the sun-lit uplands of competitive joy?

Finally, are there any demonstrable economies of scale in the business? Perhaps in part at least because of bankers' own predilection for ranking by size, outside observers cannot resist categorizing banks in some form or another on presumed economies of scale. Conventional wisdom has it, for example, that one can be a major/global/universal player who presumably enjoys some economies of scale, or one can be a niche/specialist/community bank who is high cost but offers a better service, but somehow one cannot fall between these stools.

The first response to these queries is that there are, indeed, substantial rewards for the leader in a given sector. Achieving a AAA credit rating, the proud possession of a handful of banks in the world, provides some very material benefits in the form of a lower cost of funds in the professional markets. While size is certainly not the only criterion used by the rating agencies to award this prize, it bulks large in their deliberations – if only because regulatory authorities in the major OECD countries have invariably provided support to banking institutions which are large enough to be a central element of a national banking system.

A less tangible but nonetheless understandable benefit of being at the head of the queue is image. There is marketing value in being able to say to clients and prospects that one is the largest banking institution in a given market – the assumption almost invariably being that the criterion is balance sheet size. Yet there are those that recall that the Midland Bank, which went through a time of troubles in the 1980s, was the largest bank in the world at the turn of the 19th century, and that Bank of America could make the same boast in the 1970s in the US.

The winds of change in the 1980s, however, are slowly but surely easing balance sheet size out of league table rankings in favor of profitability. The decaying value of the balance sheet as a measure of economic clout, a new generation of bankers committed to maximizing shareholder value and, in 1988, the global acceptance of standard capital adequacy ratios have swung the balance, although, like most trends in banking, the change will be a gradual one.

The most intriguing justification for achieving a given dimension, however, is that of economies of scale. This chapter will record the comments of the excellent bankers on this central issue. Suffice it to say at this point that there is an almost universal acceptance that, up to a certain point at least, amortizing central information technology and other costs over a larger business base does provide a competitive cost advantage. Given the number of occasions when such economies are trumpeted as the basis for consolidation in banking, however, the suspicious bankologist looks forward to the views of the excellent bankers to be able to separate true economies of scale from corporate public relations and desire for economic power.

Even before the Cooke Committee in 1988 reached agreement on minimum capital ratios to be applied on a risk-adjusted basis, the size of a bank's capital had generally been acknowledged as the best single measure of a bank's economic strength. Theoreticians and practitioners over the decades have debated the purpose and measurement of capital. On one memorable occasion in the 1970s Citicorp argued that the ability to raise funds in the public markets was a better barometer of strength than the existing capital base on the balance sheet. A great debate in the securities business arose at the time of Big Bang in London when the world's securities houses argued over the amount of capital required to be a global rather than simply national player in the securities business.

Our first question to the excellent banks, therefore, was how they regarded capital as a strategic concept – quite apart from whatever regulatory constraints might or might not be imposed on them. The response from S.G. Warburg, an institution at the center of the global vs. national debate, is most enlightening. Lord Garmoyle puts it as follows:

The capital argument is being made on the wrong lines. Our colleagues on the jobbing side ask themselves what they might lose on a given position vis-à-vis the potential profits. This determines how big a position to take in terms of capital. The availability of capital is not a constraining force. Liquidity and volatility are the key variables.

Such a risk-adjusted approach both to banking and securities activities is gradually being adopted by the major regulatory authorities. The end result should enable the bankologist to look beyond arbitrary absolute capital standards – in effect the RAROC principle applied for many years by Bankers Trust.

When asked about their concept of critical mass, the first response of the excellent bankers is that it is a function of the individual business segment in question. The consensus is best expressed by Dick Thomson of Toronto Dominion:

Every business has a critical mass. '

For those in the business of raising capital for prime borrowers, critical mass is easily defined: whatever the largest customer need is likely to be. William Purves of Hongkong Bank, a bold and aggressive lender for major deals, puts it simply:

Capital size is one of the two big issues along with people. I want to be able to compete for any deal if I like the credit.

Joe Manganello of Bankers Trust echoes this view:

Critical mass is the ability to do a deal from a size point of view. It gives you flexibility. It's how much shelf space you can command.

For a major universal bank like Credit Suisse, the concept is the same for a wider product range. Hans Geiger explains:

Critical mass is being sufficiently large to manage any size deal in the market.

In the retail sector, the definition is less precise but the belief in a critical threshold size is equally clear. Dick Thomson looks at critical mass from the standpoint of a major Canadian retail bank such as Toronto Dominion:

> **Size matters in the retail business. If you don't have, say, 10 per cent of the market, you can't compete unless you are incredibly innovative. It shows up in the middle market in the form of inside information on a non-public basis. Is Joe a good guy? You know who's credible.**

Below the Canadian border, John Medlin of First Wachovia agrees:

> **You have to look at individual markets and your share in them. You can be an enormous bank and be number five in each market and not make it. In the Atlanta market a toehold entry as the number five player would be just the down payment on a huge investment.**

Across the Atlantic, the numbers are not much different. Charles Green of National Westminster, Britain's largest retail bank, believes that:

> **Size is relevant to certain aspects of each business. In retail, going from 10 per cent to 20-25 per cent of the market gives you real benefits of scale.**

In the investment banking business, the universal consensus – albeit an unquantified one – is that being one of the top three to five players in most market segments is the central objective. Not only are market leaders likely to earn higher volumes and margins, but client business is understandably attracted to the leading – and presumably best qualified – players. S.G. Warburg's Lord Garmoyle believes that:

> **In a commodity business like Euro-bonds you must be one of the top three to four players. In a specialist or advisory business, one needs to be in the top three to five in a given business area.**

George Davis of Citicorp is more ambitious:

> **If you're going into a function like mergers and acquisitions, you have to be number one or two in your**

chosen niche. But there are lots of boutiques which have critical mass in one area.

For George Vojta of Bankers Trust, the concept of critical mass is much more complex:

Critical mass means relative strength across seven success factors [capital size, earning power, tradition of globalism, legal powers, technology, relative efficiency and quality of people]. If you haven't got them, don't bother to get in the business.

Moving from generalization to specifics, Tom Jones of Citicorp surveys America's largest bank's posture in different markets:

You have to look at each of the business units. Citicorp is made up of many businesses with modest market share and a few businesses with dominant market positions — like foreign exchange, bank cards and home mortgage origination. That is a real strength for us because of the opportunities for expansion in those businesses where we have modest market share.

Trying to quantify the factors behind these assumptions, however, provides no joy to the bankologist. The basic problem is the same encountered in comparing technology expenditures between banks: there are simply no reliable means of comparing apples and apples. Individual banks looking at their own numbers can see the impact of scale economies; Hilmar Kopper of Deutsche Bank describes a specific case:

We had 13 branches in Buenos Aires. The cost of putting in terminals was an expensive exercise, so we made a strategic decision to enlarge the network and bought 30 branches from Bank of America.

Behind much of the gray area in relative technology costs is the decision to make or buy a given system. Large banks in particular are prone to build a system internally. On the other hand, a growing profusion of applications systems developed and tested by market leaders such as Bankers Trust and Citicorp are being placed on the market.

Another hurdle in establishing comparability is variable expenditure on product development – particularly in the fast moving world of rate risk products. A massive expenditure on developing a new arbitrage product together with the necessary controls can provide critical mass as well as lucrative profits – or have to be written off if market conditions change or a superior product emerges.

One of the consequences of this focus on preeminence in specific markets is the awareness that selectivity is vital even for the largest banks. John Melbourn of National Westminster articulates a common view among the excellent banks:

> **NatWest is not big enough to do all it wants to do. We made a $1.2 billion acquisition in the US and would like to do more; to do it in Germany or France would be very expensive. We go where we can earn the money; we've closed or sold off operations that were too small.**

In many respects critical mass is a moving target. The needs of takeover clients for more financing for bigger deals, the growing sophistication of wealthier retail clients – all oblige the excellent bank to up the ante in different product markets. Combining this phenomenon with the understandable goal of building market share, Lord Garmoyle of S.G. Warburg puts it with tongue in cheek:

> **I've reached the conclusion that, in some businesses, critical mass is 120 per cent of where you are at the present.**

In conclusion, however difficult it is to separate economic reality from subjective considerations, gaining a certain physical share of a specific market is truly a critical success factor. The relatively small number of banks which have achieved this status in an overcrowded world is some indication of the dilemma faced even by the excellent banks. If indeed one must garner, say, at least 10 per cent of a given retail banking market and figure among the top five in a particular segment of the capital markets or wholesale banking businesses, the number of successful players in the long term is dwarfed by those presently on the playing field.

8 People: Towards the Global Meritocracy

All you have is people. – Ted McDowell, Toronto
Dominion.

The relevant chapter in *Excellence in Banking* waxed rhapsodically about the care and feeding of human resources: senior management commitment to recruitment and training, strong communications, recruiting the best and brightest, moving people around to broaden their vision and improve communication, and a reward structure that reflected cultural goals as well as performance.

Four years later, the story is the same – but with some embellishments and lessons derived from bitter experience in the battle to attract and retain the best people. This acknowledged goal of our excellent banking community is still a critical success factor – the only one in the minds of many excellent bankers who share the view of Vice Chairman Ted McDowell of Toronto Dominion:

We've finally come to realize that it's not bricks and mortar; all you have is people.

The focus of this chapter will be on the specific problems of attracting and retaining superior people in an environment of change. Readers of *Excellence in Banking* – or for that matter any text on human resource management – know the party line on the does and dont's of good human resource management. What, however, are the specific problems excellent banks face in today's environment, and how are they addressing them?

The first problem is that posed by the massive influx of specialist professionals in what used to be a generalist's world. The common cultural bonds of growing up together as trainees and moving through a series of line and staff functions have frayed in the face of the need to recruit specialists who do not share – and perhaps do not care to share – this heritage.

George Davis of Citicorp expresses the problem graphically:

> **You require different types of people: it's high tech intermediation. They're not account officers but deal technicians – a series of product specialists trained to do arcane financial transactions. There's room for the generalist, but it's different than it once was. Relationship is still the name of the game, but relationship today may give you only the right to *bid*, not the right to *get* the business.**

Bob Engel of J.P. Morgan observes the same phenomenon:

> **You have to have a skill and build on it. You can have a rewarding career by being a specialist or a generalist. But specialization will be the focus early in the career. The opportunity is there to switch.**

The dilemma created for human resource management is a serious one. The manifold virtues of moving high potential people from job to job to carry less weight when a highly paid specialist is recruited to do a very specific task. Does one try to integrate such a specialist in the bank's overall career path structure – quite apart from reconciling widely different compensation structures?

The response at Citicorp is essentially positive. Pam Flaherty, head of Citicorp's human resource function, describes the approach:

> **We're hiring more specialists than ever before, especially as we acquire new businesses. We're learning how to manage specialists and staff in existing businesses. Integrating people into the corporate culture, however, is a two way street; we need to change as well.**

Not surprisingly, incentive compensation is proving to be the fulcrum against which much of the tension from external change is directed. Virtually any conversation with an excellent banker on the subject of people turns eventually to managing the process of awarding incentive compensation and the key role of performance evaluation.

Strategic and cultural goals are interwoven with the incentive compensation process. At S.G. Warburg with its strong commitment to shared values, personnel head Hugh Stevenson outlines his experience:

We have a firm-wide bonus but also a special bonus on top. You simply can't be totally fair in this business. But it helps that we're all in it together.

His colleague Peter Wilmot Sitwell echoes the commitment to a firm-wide approach:

I passionately believe in a single bonus pool; don't divisionalize the bonus. We're all working for each other.

For the excellent banks who want to reward individual performance yet still retain shared goals and reinforce elements of a common culture, the solution is an extended dialogue involving heavy amounts of senior management time. Urban Joseph of Toronto Dominion lists the objectives:

There are two objectives: we want more people to be proprietors, and the variable compensation plan will emphasize individual as well as team performance. Team effort, bank performance and time are variables. The five Executive Vice Presidents and the President allocate the bank's variable compensation to all officers. It creates lots of cooperation; there's more agreement than disagreement.

A similar philosophy shapes the incentive compensation dialogue at Bankers Trust. Mark Bieler summarizes:

The Management Committee gets together – a partnership of people in the midst of the deal flow. They ask questions like 'does he collaborate'. We try to destroy the concept that any profit center 'owns' its own pool.

But there is still pain involved even in the best of compensation systems. Chairman Lew Preston of J.P. Morgan tracks the impact of incentive compensation for specialists:

This change has been hard at a bank which belittles profit centers except as a management tool. You need

to get the best people – yet that endangers our 'one bank' philosophy.[1]

While the excellent European banks also pay their investment bankers on an incentive basis, they have not yet integrated their commercial bankers into such programs. Ulrich Weiss of Deutsche Bank describes the approach:

> **There's still a distinction between people paid on performance and the classical relationship manager. For the typical investment banker, there are more people with limited contracts where the performance component can be two or three times the fixed element. Deutsche Bank Capital Markets runs its business on its own rules. If the market moves to more integration, it may become a bigger problem.**

Another focus of attention is the role being played by the younger generation – more technologically literate, less willing to fit into traditional structures, amd much better educated than the current generation of senior managers. Toronto Dominion's Urban Joseph describes what he considers the principal issue facing Canadian banks:

> **Canadian banks grew up with high school graduates. Thousands of these will leave the work force in the 1980s and 1990s. The banks replacing them with better educated people will be the leaders. The issue is thus the upgrading of the workforce. We're going through a paradigm shift. Will the empty spaces be replaced by better people; not everyone is doing it.**

The current top management of the banks built on people who joined in their teens – school leavers in Britain, apprentices in Switzerland and Germany – is well aware of the potential – and the demands – of their successors. Tom Frost of National Westminster exudes excitement:

> **I'd bet our younger people against any others in the world. My successor will be a double graduate, I have no doubt. The younger they are, the better they are. The cultural change is not easy, but they're challenged according to perceived capability. We've managed the**

friction by building bridges; the bridges are there for proven excellence.

An evening with a group of young Zurich bankers reveals an iconoclastic, meritocratic view of their employer together with a marked disdain for organizational boundaries and the territorial mentality which often accompanies them. Robert Jeker of Credit Suisse describes a recent conference bringing together hundreds of his managers:

> **Our youth is our key strength. We had five of the younger managers come to the floor to describe publicly what they would change if they were at the top. They were free to say what they wanted; we listened and will follow up.**

At Toronto Dominion Bank, Dick Thomson lauds the capabilities of his younger managers:

> **Young people love it [the absence of policies]; they think of change all the time. They keep asking 'why is it so slow'. They make me realize we're not changing fast enough.**

Another issue raised by environmental change is the need to manage the ambiguities of a matrix organization. Like their American counterparts, the other excellent banks have been compelled by increasing product and client focus to work with more complex lines of reporting responsibilities. For Hans-Ulrich Doerig, whose capital market responsibilities at Credit Suisse involve managing both product and relationship officers, it is all part of the management job:

> **It's a tough problem. In good markets, the product people are up; in bad times, it's the reverse. From time to time, some product guys need their heads examined. I have to bring them both down to earth from time to time. It's a question of communication and being realistic. They both have needs. It's up to management to calm them down, to provide an equilibrium, to get them in the same room. You have to make public examples of what one has done to help the others. You have to find out what the client is – is he relationship or product oriented.**

His colleague Robert Jeker agrees on the importance of communication:

> **It's a question of how you want to succeed. We have a formal matrix, but the key is to have an open flow of information and an understanding of the importance of information. It should then work informally.**

Across the street at Union Bank of Switzerland, Mathis Cabiallavetta acknowledges the natural tensions involved:

> **At UBS we follow the matrix system. For example, I have both some line managers and a function reporting to me. Obviously at times it is prone to tension, but that is exactly what it is designed to do. One gets the checks and balances from the ideas from both product and line managers.**

At Bankers Trust, Mark Bieler makes the same point:

> **No one can completely resolve the tension between product and relationship. Historically, banks' emphasis has been on relationships. In recent years, Bankers Trust has tilted toward product. The question is how to provide an effective balance so that product can help build stronger relationships and those stronger relationships position you to provide more products.**

For an institution with a strong tradition of shared values and of moving people around in line and staff jobs, the management task is less difficult. Charles Green of National Westminster Bank explains how the matrix is part of NatWest's culture:

> **The matrix is built around a lifetime career structure. It's not a cultural shock to move through the organization. For a specialist like a swaps expert, we pay the price, but it's not a career. The culture hasn't actually changed. In the future, we'll be increasingly challenged to get the bright minds, but with personalities which are durable.**

On the other hand, the massive influx of specialists needed by the North American banks places severe limits on management's ability to oil the matrix process by internal transfer.

Urban Joseph of Toronto Dominion repeats a point made by his peers in the US money center banks:

Employees can have outstanding careers without being good managers. Every department participates in the variable compensation plan. Now you can make a full career in a product specialty. You don't have to be a manager to get paid well.

The impact of change has reinforced some of the themes highlighted in *Excellence in Banking*. Communication is one of them. In a vast retail organization such as National Westminster, getting a new message across entails an equally extensive communication effort. Roger Flemington recounts their experience:

Bringing sales people up front in the branches to build client relationships was a bit of a cultural shock. We took the whole branch staff through a quality service program as a part of the communication process. There was a fair amount of criticism. The real core of interest was in what NatWest is doing and why. It was 'want to know', not 'need to know'. We opened up Pandora's Box, but it's natural – we're in the relationship business.

Bankers Trust's Mark Bieler emphasizes the need for clarity and honesty in a rapidly changing organization:

People are smarter than management. You can't fool them. They'll pick up the difference between what you do and what you say. It's a question of action. People are watching. People will put up with tougher performance standards if they understand the strategy.

The same honesty applies to the compensation process. Credit Suisse's Hans-Ulrich Doerig explains:

I assume the salary scales of my people will be published tomorrow. Can I justify the differences? How would I handle objections?

Central to the human resource function in a rapidly changing world is the performance evaluation function. This time consuming and often culturally challenging process is easily pushed to the bottom of an in-box, yet the signals it sends are vital to the process of managing change. Pam Flaherty of Citicorp discusses how it works:

> **The manpower review process is a logical way to reinforce corporate values – and by making it a process we can make sure that this happens. Staff people can sometimes feel good about paper files and reports, but what really makes the difference is that management takes responsibility for developing people. It's all about taking risks on people and stretching them. A good process doesn't have to be bureaucratic. Management commitment sends big signals through the organization. It doesn't escape people's attention that when John Reed goes into a manpower review meeting he does not allow any interruptions.**

The review process also serves as a communications device in organizations faced with great diversity and the problem of building management skills. Credit Suisse uses the technique of management assessment centers for a variety of purposes. Joerg Mueller, First Vice President in the personnel function, explains how it works:

> **Ten years ago, if you got promoted to Vice President, you kept the title until you retired. Now we have to pay attention to potential performance before we make the promotion. We started assessment centers and have put 600 people through them. We've created a style of assessing at Credit Suisse. There are always four senior line officers as assessors. We now use the same language. If you're a branch manager in Zurich and you've seen a branch manager from Geneva being assessed, maybe you understand why one of your own people shouldn't be promoted. It gives management an opportunity to see people deal with real problems. In most cases the feedback is accepted – 'Nobody told me that before'.**

The challenge of creating and maintaining an entrepreneurial environment is foremost in the minds of the excellent bankers – in particular those competing for the best and brightest across a vast array of specialty functions. The vertical hierarchy and consensus decision-making process of traditional banking are formidable obstacles. Hans-Joerg Rudloff of Credit Suisse First Boston articulates the ideal:

> **We push the individual to perform. If you run the French country desk, your job is build a reputation as their advisor. It's a lifetime job to become the number one banker to a client. With that system of independent businesses, we have no hierarchy problem. People don't have the ambition to become the CEO. In a bank, everything is linked to your position in the hierarchy. Here people are powerful through their own franchise. With the hierarchy problem out of the way, we can hire many more good people. Here they have a lot of leeway to run their businesses the way they feel it fits best to a specific country.**

Achieving this ideal is an effort for the US money center banks.

For Bob Engel of J.P. Morgan, it is one of the two principal issues facing a bank like Morgan:

> **It's making sure that you continue to have an entre-preneurial environment.**

At Citicorp, the answer is decentralization and diversity, with a willingness to take risks on people. Chairman John Reed articulates the philosophy:

> **We recruit around the world with a very active campaign to recruit everybody – I mean everybody. Since we really do believe we are a meritocracy, we really do not care where you went to school. We try to identify talent early and move people around so that the talent surfaces. It's a culture that says 'Take chances on people'.[2]**

For Bankers Trust, the goal is a flatter structure in keeping with its Wall Street peers. Charlie Sanford articulates the philosophy:

> **I don't want to run this place like an army, where everyone is fungible. I'd rather pattern my organization after a theatre company or opera. I see the people we are trying to attract and retain as more like artists or musicians. They are a talented group and they deserve**

to be treated that way. Say you hired Pavarotti and Sutherland, and you said to Pavarotti, 'Lou, maybe you sell more tickets, but you still report to Joan'. How long would you keep Pavarotti? Not long, for damn sure.[3]

The same sense of entrepreneurship – within a strong culture – lies behind much of the success of the S.G. Warburg merger. Peter Wilmot Sitwell explains:

> **The lesson of our experience is that you have to allow the component parts to manage themselves. You have to make people feel responsible for their own area.**

Managing bright, entrepreneurial spirits is a challenge for a highly structured commercial bank and falls heavily on the shoulders of the chief executive. Robert Jeker describes the process of building such a management team over his period as CEO:

> **We want the best people. We are receptive to new ideas. All the new people in top management have their own ideas; we didn't take the easy ones! I can't live with people who say 'yes', and they don't feel comfortable with me. It's more demanding, but I concentrate on the most important issues – strategy, business philosophy, etc. – then let people go, with much more authority.**

What emerges from all these inputs from banks at different stages of development is an inexorable trend towards a global meritocracy. What fascinates anyone observing an organization from the outside is the perceived degree of 'politics' – the level of internal friction, of cliques built around power bases. For the excellent bankers, meritocracy is the antithesis of politics. In a meritocracy, an individual is utilized, rewarded and promoted on the basis of his agreed worth and ability to contribute to the bank's strategic goals.

Moving toward this meritocratic nirvana must thus be the central challenge for the excellent banks in the human resource dimension. Complicating it are the need to integrate product specialists and, for those committed to geographic expansion into different markets, the issue of national and other cultures. A bank like Citicorp moving ahead on all these fronts thus is at the forefront of the struggle.

Pam Flaherty sums it up:

> **We've recognized that people are our greatest strength
> and greatest challenge. People depth in the broadest
> context is our greatest challenge. We're more com-
> fortable than most with managing a vast multinational
> organization, but it's still a challenge. We still have a
> way to go to become more multi-cultural.**

For an organization like a major Swiss bank with a
strong national culture yet equally powerful ambitions in
overseas markets, there is arguably a greater distance to
travel. Mathis Cabiallavetta of Union Bank of Switzerland
cites this as the principal issue facing UBS:

> **The key is getting the right people. One needs to attract
> the best. We shall be successful when we can attract the
> best local people and meld them with our own standard
> of efficiency and productivity. Everything else then falls
> into place. We can see the first results clearly. But in
> general it will take five years before it all functions.**

Deutsche Bank also has a distance to travel. Hilmar Kopper
likens it to turning a battleship:

> **We have to reassess our strategy. It has to start at the
> top. Our culture should be an international one, mov-
> ing to becoming multi-national. We want good people
> – we don't care about passports. But it's like a big
> battleship. In our bank we don't blow a whistle and
> everything changes.**

Once again, that issue of *time* – of having sufficient patience
to build the necessary human resources – just as it takes
time to bring cultures together, to obtain critical mass and
upgrade information technology. Do banks have the time or,
a more relevant point, will they take the time?

Behind so much of the response of non – US excellent
banks is the not-so-hidden conviction that their US peers
are driven too much by short term considerations such as
quarterly earnings per share results. Can a US bank make the
necessary investment in human and technological resources
over a decade or more to position itself in a changing market
place? Chapter 11 will attempt to address this nagging doubt.

9 The Management Factor

Leadership is showing the way; it's ensuring a vision my colleagues can share. – Tom Frost, National Westminster.

The third factor which will differentiate excellent banks in the future from their less successful peers will be the quality of management. In one sense this is a truism, a statement of the obvious. But management quality underlies all of the other success factors – building critical mass, attracting and retaining the right people, and setting the institution on the right strategic course. It is, in effect, what this book has been all about. And it is the pace of change and management's ability to deal with it which is separating the banking sheep from the goats.

What do we mean by management as a success factor? How do we recognize successful management from the less happy alternative? In a word, by its ability to manage change – to address successfully all of the issues debated in this volume. What distinguished the regulated institutions of the past from today's banking environment is that a regulated institution could be administered within a set of prescribed guidelines. Today's animal must be managed like any other deregulated business under attack from all sides and suffering from massive overcapacity.

How do we start to address the issue of successful management qualities? As so many excellent bankers have suggested, by starting at the top with leadership. *Excellence in Banking* devoted Chapter 7 to the leadership of these superior institutions. Its conclusions were that strong, consistent leadership transmitting a simple message throughout the organization was the distinguishing feature of these banks. Management *style* – autocratic, democratic or federal – was of secondary significance.

We asked the chief executives and their senior colleagues to describe the role of leadership in addressing the issues associated with change. The responses centred on one theme: to establish and communicate the values which would guide the bank in its new environment. Robert Jeker of Credit Suisse expresses the view of many of his peers:

> **My most important task is to let people feel what the corporate culture of Credit Suisse is – and what won't change in the future. The markets are changing, but the quality of service won't change. Competence, speed and friendliness are the three key tasks for Credit Suisse management. I'll personally talk to managers when something is excellent or not.**

Tom Frost at National Westminster expresses a similar view:

> **Leadership is showing the way – in different forms. It means bringing together the thought processes of all my colleagues, of pointing us all in the right direction, and from time to time adding a touch on the tiller. It's ensuring a vision they can share. I've spoken recently to all 6500 managers and shared that vision with them. If they're on board, progress can't be stopped. The success of National Westminster has been getting the crew to face the same way. I have to tune the motor.**

Vision is also central to Charlie Sanford's leadership at Bankers Trust:

> **I think I have a feel of how this industry's going to go. We're not just taking the average of what everybody else thinks. We'll do what we think, and we're going to show leadership in that sense.[1]**

The theme of communication is vital to William Purves's concept of leadership at Hongkong Bank:

> **Leadership means being in touch – communication. You have to find the time. The team has to be able to beard you in a corner and not get their heads chopped off. The key players in the organization should have no trouble in picking up the telephone if something needs to be said. You get it best when you're consistent; the team needs to know where they stand – that when the chips are down, you'll listen. You have to develop and encourage the newcomers; it takes time for them to feel comfortable.**

Sir David Scholey's role in the merger process at S.G. Warburg reflects another dimension of leadership. As a Warburg colleague recalls:

> **Scholey attended all the meetings and put his personal stamp on the whole process, but he never forced his will on people.[2]**

At First Wachovia, John Medlin emphasizes some of the more difficult aspects of being a visionary in a time of rapid change:

> **Leadership is preserving and espousing the philosophy. You're something of a visionary; leadership means being a little lonely, especially when you stick to principles and aren't attracted to fads and fashions like LBOs. When you're already excellent, the biggest challenge is to maintain it. There's an adrenalin flow to get you there, but what do you do to keep the people inspired?**

For Hans-Joerg Rudloff at Credit Suisse First Boston, the inspirational role in a difficult market environment is the hallmark of leadership:

> **You have to provide excitement. Our people are all foreigners; they all want to go back where they came from. To make them stay, you have to give them pride in what they're doing. In the 1980s, history was written in the international capital markets. They've been part of history being made.**

Dick Thomson of Toronto Dominion expresses a more flexible approach to setting standards:

> **There are no ten rules of leadership. It's setting the tone – like 'slow and steady wins the race'. My involvement is heavily weighted toward people, policies and what happens when things go wrong. For example, how do you handle discipline. What encouragement do you give to long term growth vs. short term gain?**

From these guidelines as well as the mass of evidence reflected in earlier quotations in this book, it is clear that establishing and propagating shared values appropriate to the new environment is a central mission of management.

The dilemma faced by so many excellent banks in *Excellence in Banking* was that their culture was indeed rich in shared values, but those values were not necessarily appropriate for a world of change. The principal casualty – particularly for the non-North American institutions – has been the family feeling: the commitment to care for all members of the corporate family throughout their career.

The family is truly under siege as the excellent banks, one by one, move towards the ideal of a meritocracy. Management's task has thus been the delicate one of emphasizing the appropriate common values: communication; providing independent, quality advice; decentralization and diversity, and the like – while at the same time making it crystal clear that new skills and performance standards are needed.

Getting the balance right between the good old values and the tough new ones is thus one of the litmus paper tests of excellent bank management. One hears it constantly in the reference to the need for a common language. Victor Menezes of Citicorp puts it neatly:

> **The challenge in our bank – and the industry in general – is language. It's defining what constitutes success and performance. It used to be the size of the balance sheet. If 'success' is what motivates people, what should our definition be of 'success'? It's a mosaic of many things; it doesn't boil down to a simple number. It's the toughest part of managing change. I'm not convinced the market gives you signals.**

When the common language is accepted, however, the results are gratifying. In a banking institution like First Wachovia whose values have remained constant despite the changing environment, there is positive reinforcement. Bud Baker at First Wachovia describes how a senior credit officer reacts to change:

> **We've had a fundamental change in the lending environment. During such times we have to come back to anchor posts – our belief in balance in management and excellent people.**

Implementing change in a fashion consistent with cultural values is one solution. Roger Flemington of National

Westminster recounts how a major restructuring of the bank's core retail business took place:

> **The challenge is to be sure change has the right fit – that it falls within the broad range of our particular culture, which is strength and success through teamwork. It's a collegiate style – it sounds odd, but that's how it works. We've reorganized headquarters supervision to produce a shorter decision making chain; the old area director has gone. And we've centralized on two streams of personal and commercial business.**

Toronto Dominion has also successfully channeled change within the framework of strong cultural values. Dick Thomson explains how their investment banking strategy is built on these values:

> **We're turning corporate bankers into securities people; they come from the same talent pool of people in their late 20s and 30s. We're going to make it one culture. It will be slow, but people are excited about it. Selling paper requires a lot of trust – the willingness of the retail operators to give access to others without a fight. The only way to win is for the whole bank to succeed.**

For other excellent banks, however, existing cultural values still represent an obstacle to change. Peter Brockman of HongkongBank explains:

> **In managing change, we have no problem with innovations, but we still do with the structure of the organization: would change endanger the culture? We debate on a continuing basis whether to broaden management recruitment, which has been almost exclusively out of the UK. We're no longer a regional bank in a British colony; we should have an international expatriate cadre. Our culture is such a strong one, and what is unifying is the culture in which you grow up.**

John Reed of Citicorp agrees that the existing culture in many respects drives strategy. Referring to Citicorp's absence from the middle market corporate sector, he explains:

The requirements for success in that business seem to be out of whack with the requirements of our culture. It requires long term continuity of people who are part of the local community, and we tend to be a bunch of nomads who run around the world. We do not attract university graduates who want to go to Kenosha, Wisconsin, and live there for 25 years.[3]

The argument is put most frankly by another bank whose culture is changing   Deutsche Bank. Hilmar Kopper refers to the current discussions on strategy:

Culture is an ever-changing animal. Culture shouldn't be used as an excuse for not moving in a changing environment. Part of our culture is to stay ahead. Some items will remain forever – like integrity and loyalty to our people and clients.

A second theme of successful management of change is achieving the appropriate balance between entrepreneurship and discipline. Banks have traditionally been very good at the latter, if only because survival has been a function of rigorous risk assessment carried out in an environment of strong checks and balances. As for entrepreneurship, all the excellent banks trumpet the virtues of delegation of authority, attracting top people and letting them get on with the job. Yet the tensions of these two great tectonic plates moving together are foremost on the minds of management at frontrunners such as Citicorp and Bankers Trust.

At Citicorp, for example, one hears the word 'discipline' mentioned frequently. Larry Glenn draws together many of the threads:

The culture is changing towards more focussed business units and specialists who are very product oriented: As a result you're short of the wisdom needed to be a general manager. I worry about it a lot. There are no answers; it's an issue of functional organization. You need clear cut rules and precepts on how to manage traders, for example. You have to keep it in proportion.

A friend at J.P. Morgan observes the paradox produced by the trend toward specialization:

The rise of specialization comes at a time when you need greater teamwork. It's like oil and water – an inherent contradiction. With a functional orientation, people think of their own bottom line. The conclusion is that you need general goals but flexibility of interpretation.

Related to this tradeoff between flexibility and critical mass, as Bob Engel of J.P. Morgan puts it, is that of managing diversity. When *Excellence in Banking* was written, the debate in many excellent institutions was between those who felt they could maintain a single set of common values, or culture, and those who acknowledged that different cultures were inherent in their business strategy. The world has moved on, and there is now general recognition that the issue is how to manage people with diverse backgrounds yet maintain certain core, common and relevant values.

The leadership challenge is thus to get this diverse mix of skills and backgrounds moving in the same direction. Managing the resulting tensions becomes the principal challenge. Victor Menezes of Citicorp, which is arguably the most diverse of the excellent banks, acknowledges the difficulty:

We do find a certain bit of tension. If we had a more narrowly focussed business, the tension would be much less. I'm afraid that tension comes from being decentralized and entrepreneurial – not from being multinational.

Bankers Trust has been a laboratory of change over the past decade. Mark Bieler draws his own conclusions:

The issue is cultural balance. We struggle with it. There's a continuum ranging from highly collaborative to adversarial. Historically Bankers Trust has functioned at the collaborative end. As you tighten standards, put a lot of money on the table, and bring in scads of new people – lots of Pharoahs who knew not Joseph, there can be an inexorable drift toward the adversarial side. We don't want to lose our bearings. We need to find ways to deal with real conflict. We let it happen and deal with it honestly. For example, we used outsiders to grow a separate corporate finance entity. It flourished, but the conflicts grew, and we absorbed it into the rest of the

business with very few people at the top leaving. Management is the ability to create and manage conflict.

Another crucible of change for the excellent banks in recent years has been the merger process, in particular interstate banking in the US. What lessons in managing change can be drawn from this experience? Charles Thayer, Executive Vice President of PNC Financial Corporation, recounts how PNC has integrated key executives of its merger partners:

> We spent a lot of time looking at the people managing the potential acquisition candidates. There is a visible strategy of maintaining the name of the company and its ownership of its customers. What is less visible is a lot of effort to rationalize support services. Merging cultures starts at the top; look at who makes up the PNC management committee – the former CEOs of the component banking groups merged. They wear two hats. At the staff level, we've found that with geographic diversity, it's not necessary for all senior people to live in the same city and work in the same building.

Communication and honesty in the merger process are vital. Charles Thayer continues:

> The biggest fear among people in a merger is that their career paths might be constrained. If they can see their's broadened, you'll keep the good people. The good people get the headhunter's telephone calls. We tell them what's going to happen. There are no surprises. The worst thing you can do is the proverbial song and dance, then have a different story afterward.

For First Wachovia, the principal merger lesson is the importance of time in dealing with the human dimension of change. John Medlin explains:

> You start with the realization that banks are nothing more than people – customers and employees. We had to go through the process without losing these people. There's a balance between human sensitivity and business urgency. It can cost more to do things too quickly; it takes more time to do them properly. We left symbols of the past – we didn't change the name, for example.

The theme of patience in dealing with change is articulated
by a wide variety of excellent bankers. Bankers Trust's
transformation has taken a decade under forceful, consistent leadership.

At Toronto Dominion, one of Dick Thomson's aphorisms
is 'slow and steady wins the game':

> **How do you effect change? Some people visualize the
> CEO as sitting behind a desk with five buttons and
> six levers. It's more like pushing carefully and gen-
> tly on a string. When we decide that we're going
> to effect a major change in our organization, we do
> it incrementally, carefully and slowly – so that it is
> understood by the people affected in the organization.**

At HongkongBank, Stephen Green, who runs the group
treasury, describes the process by which the various capital
market elements of the group are getting together:

> **People are key in the matrix process. The philosophy
> is 'let the logic let it happen'.**

Another friend at HongkongBank, which has sustained
its tradition of federalism in a functional age, refers to
a Schopenhauer quotation on human balance:

> **People are like porcupines huddling together for
> warmth. You hope you find the right distance; if
> you're too close, you get pricked; if you're too
> far apart, you get cold.**

One of the lessons of the excellent banks' experience,
not surprisingly, is that a history of having dealt with
change is a valuable asset in the current environment.
At S.G. Warburg, the frontier spirit is alive and well,
as Lord Garmoyle describes:

> **We're a young, postwar organization. There's no feeling
> that we were always there. No one owes us a living.**

A tradition of living with change has value even among
the more mature national commercial banks. Bill Brock
looks back at the history of Toronto Dominion:

We merged two different cultures in 1955. The management philosophy then was 'we have to accept change'. When adverse market conditions hit us in the 1980s, our people were more prepared than the others.

At National Westminster, John Burns, the Chief Financial Officer and a General Manager, expresses the same view:

We went through a big merger in the early 1970s; there was a tremendous upheaval. Out of it emerged a new bank – a new culture. We drew the best from both components; we've got a long history of managing change. Now we've reshaped totally the domestic business and have had to carry some 55,000 staff with us.

Another hallmark of successful management of change is the willingness to recruit, train and promote highly qualified members of the younger generation of bankers. This feisty band, as noted in Chapter 8, has already made its mark in institutions such as Credit Suisse, Toronto Dominion and National Westminster. Charles Thayer of PNC puts the people factor in a historical perspective:

The most important success factor for the future is the selection of people. As a regulated industry, we didn't attract the best and the brightest. The banking companies that will be the most successful will search the organization for the best people; if they don't find them, they'll have the courage to look outside for talent.

To sum up the success factor of managing change, once again the guidelines are reasonably clear. Select and drive home the values that can unite an increasingly diverse team. Support entrepreneurship but ensure that some form of discipline is a cherished value. Place an even higher priority on communication and honesty in addressing the stresses which will inevitably arise. Be patient; acknowledge that people take time to adjust to new realities. And make meritocracy one of your values – especially if you want to infuse a traditional organization with young, more talented blood.

And the result? An imperfect process in which having all the troops marching in the same direction is a mark of success. At Bankers Trust, which has been embarked on the process since the mid-1970s, Mark Bieler looks back at the process of assimilating different cultures in the bank:

> **Don't grind down or shatter individual cultures; bring them in on a phased basis. As an analogy, the United States isn't a melting pot; it's really more of a beef stew whose separate ingredients are still discernible in the whole.**

10 Strategic Positioning: The Shape of Things to Come

The fourth, and last, vital success factor for banks in a changing world is the quality of their strategy. This chapter will summarize the author's views on what will constitute the essential elements of such a strategy. It will also address some of the central issues faced by banks in making strategic choices and, finally, paint a picture of the likely banking horizon which will emerge from these strategic decisions.

Chapter 6 highlighted the priority being given to strategic positioning by banks which heretofore, as our friend at J.P. Morgan put it, had previously been operating on automatic pilot. It might be useful here to define our terms and, drawing on the author's own experience as a strategic planning consultant to banking institutions, describe how banks actually address the process.

While there is a broad array of definitions, 'strategy' for most banks means long term competitive positioning. It focusses, particularly in a business swimming in overcapacity, on establishing and maintaining a competitive advantage in one or more businesses which can be used to earn an acceptable rate of return on shareholders' funds.

Now comes the hard part. What constitutes a competitive advantage? For a bank with a major nationwide consumer franchise, it is relatively easy: a potentially lucrative distribution network built around core banking relationships with individual and small/medium sized corporate customers. For others with an acknowledged product advantage, such as a leading Swiss bank in managing assets in the conservative Swiss tradition or an investment bank such as Credit Suisse First Boston with a reputation for product leadership on a vast scale, the task is also relatively straightforward.

But for a bank operating outside its natural client franchise, say, in a foreign market, or as a secondary supplier of product in its own market, the job gets tougher. The temptation then is to articulate criteria which are extraordinarily difficult to quantify or relate to a competitor's capability. Quality, for instance. Or people. What does 'quality' mean; is it speed of service, absence of errors, or simply image? Bankers all acknowledge the need for superior people, yet how can you compare your paragons with the competition? And, for a national bank with operations and ambitions abroad, how important to your home country customers is it to have your branch on the spot – especially since most surveys show that a home country affiliate abroad usually prefers to bank with local institutions because the local competitor has more product, distribution or expertise to offer.

The danger, therefore, is that the wish becomes father to the thought. In strategy statements one sees phrases like 'offer superior products', 'high quality people skills' and 'broad range of services' which may be technically correct but are not only extremely difficult to quantify but also less than inspiring as a battle cry to one's team. A typical mission statement for a major national bank with overseas operations will thus 'offer a full range of financial services to our domestic clientele and a selected range to overseas clients'. True that may be as a statement of fact, but it often leaves something to be desired as a conscientious analysis of exactly what represents a long term competitive advantage. The bankologist thus usually needs to descend to the level of the three central dimensions of any banking institution's inner workings – product, client and geographic – to learn what makes the bank's strategy really tick.

At the level of client base, at one extreme is the national bank with millions of primary relationships with individual retail clients. Excellent national banks such as National Westminster, Toronto Dominion and Deutsche Bank thus enjoy what has been the most lucrative business base of the 1980s: a distribution network which enables the bank to tap the core deposits and daily transactions of an increasingly affluent base of individual and small/medium sized corporate clients. The same benefits accrue to franchises at the regional or community level – but on a smaller scale. For these banks the challenge has been to distribute a growing array of non-traditional products – securities, insurance, asset management and various forms of consumer finance – both to satisfy expanding client needs and to offset the surging costs of technology. For these players, the nightmare is the threat of a cheaper delivery system. The good news, however, is that these relationships rarely move as long as the bank provides acceptable service and an up-to date product array. As Charles Thayer of PNC puts it:

People move accounts because the bank screws up. Happy customers don't move – it takes too much effort.

For a securities firm like Credit Suisse First Boston or S.G. Warburg, the client base is a less well defined but nonetheless central core of the business strategy. While many issuers and other corporate clients have preferred relationships with one or more securities houses, by and large transactions are earned on a one-off basis by the quality of service or product advantage: price, placing power, innovation, identification of target counterpart, or other tangible feature. Credibility is key to initiating a relationship – a barrier which commercial banks such as J.P. Morgan and Bankers Trust have hurdled.

At the product level, competitive advantage has been gained in recent years largely in the rate risk management sector in which a limited number of largely Anglo-Saxon investment and commercial banks have taken the lead through innovation and the use of technology. Leverage financing techniques, mergers and acquisitions and other high value-added products in the corporate sector have been given high priority. For the consumer, product advantage has been defined more in terms of broadening the array by borrowing products developed in other markets: deposit accounts tied to money market rates, insurance or asset management products, mortgages and the like.

In the geographic dimension, banks have largely been frustrated in their efforts to expand into new markets through start-up operations – whether across national boundaries or simply outside their natural client franchises. Core retail and corporate relationships in a variety of attractive markets have proved extraordinarily difficult to move, and the newcomer has generally been required to buy business as a marginal supplier or limit himself to a narrow range of products such as mortgages and credit cards. The virtues of global coverage trumpeted by US banks such as Citicorp and Chase Manhattan have thus often proven deceptive, and considerable trimming of both large and small international networks has been executed by these and other banks which are particularly sensitive to the short and medium term profit outlook.

Given these conditions – which obtain in most of the national markets of interest to major banks – the generic strategic options open to banking institutions are fundamentally twofold:

– **Buy a client franchise through an acquisition:** this has taken place when artificial entry barriers come down as in the case of interstate banking in the US or Big Bang in the UK. It also occurs when a weakened bank, directly or indirectly, is obliged to sell an interest in an attractive franchise; examples here include the HongkongBank's strategic investment in Midland Bank and the sale of Banca d'America e d'Italia to Deutsche Bank. Such deals are facilitated when the financial leverage in terms of premium over book value or enhanced earnings per share is highly attractive to buyer or seller.

– **Buy or build internally product strength which can be marketed to a wider client base or at a premium return:** this strategy has been followed by the US money center banks which have lacked a sufficient retail/small corporate franchise. It has also been a strategic objective of commercial banks with such a franchise but aware of the limited profit potential in their marketplace; thus US superregionals like First Wachovia and PNC are devoting considerable resources to building a nationwide leadership position in products such as cash management, mutual fund processing and other areas where their technology or expertise gives them a competitive advantage.

While the acquisition alternative has manifold attractions, in practice the opportunities are limited by cultural barriers (as perceived by both buyer and seller), resistance by local regulatory and other authorities, and the limited number of stockholder-owned banks which are perceived by potential buyers to be attractive. Banks combing European markets in anticipation of the single European market after 1992 have thus found precious few such customer franchises which do not require a top-to-bottom restructuring by local management – which the buyers rarely have in depth. Yet most of the limited number of successful retail franchises operated by foreign banks in Europe stem from acquisitions – such as Citicorp's purchase of Kundenkreditbank in Germany and Deutsche Bank's acquisition of Banca d'America e d'Italia.

So for most banking institutions around the world, the driving force for their strategy is product – either to be sold to an existing customer base, to earn profits from an innovative edge, or to garner new clients. In terms of the excellent banks, PNC would be a case study of the former: cross selling an established product to a client base broadened by acquisition. Bankers Trust is using its innovative leveraged lending and rate risk management products as a profit center, while Citicorp is chasing new clients on the basis of its product capabilities in credit cards, mortgage lending, and foreign exchange.

From these basic assumptions two trends are emerging. First, the increase in differentiation. If the experience of regional and superregional banks in the US is any indication of the outlook for other commercial banking institutions, thoughtful banks will focus increasingly on products in which they can gain a competitive advantage. Our interviews with banks like First Wachovia and PNC confirm that, even for the most successful commercial banking customer franchise, the competitive pressures from investment banks at the top end and cost pressures in the traditional products are driving them towards product specialization. In the US the extreme cases are banks like Banc One and State Street of Boston which have largely given up a traditional banking activity in favor of a specialist data processing function.

A corollary of this differentiation is that the ultimate specialization may have little or nothing to do with traditional commercial banking.

Asset management, data processing, cash management, mortgage banking – all constitute viable alternatives to taking deposits and lending money. A parallel exists in the securities business where firms have found competitive the securities business where firms have found competitive advantage in mergers and acquisitions, fixed interest or equity placements, or money management.

A second trend is the increasing differentiation between client-driven and product-driven banking institutions. Most European and Asian banks have splendid strength in providing a broad array of competitive products to their traditional clientele, but have little in the way of products which can be marketed competitively outside this market. With sufficient introspection and investment, they may develop such a capability, but in the last analysis they are likely to find that their competitive advantage lies in acting as a distribution channel to their existing clientele.

By the same token, more banks may emulate the investment banking institution whose raison d'etre is product strength. The three US money center banks which make up the excellent banking community in New York are all essentially product-driven and will rise or fall on their ability to compete on product innovation, price or quality. In the commercial banking sector, cash management or data processing could constitute the same product advantage.

As this global trend toward differentiation proceeds, a number of issues are posed. The first, which was addressed in Chapter 7, is that of size and critical mass. Is there any particular magic in being a so-called regional bank or one with, say, $10 billion equivalent in assets? The response of our excellent banks was quite specific in this respect: aggregate size has little significance in comparison to relative market position in one or more specific businesses – with the exception of the relative handful of institutions who need a capital base to handle the very largest individual transactions. The strategic response, therefore, should be to gear one's physical size and capital needs to the total of businesses in which one can achieve critical mass. The end result, in many respects, will be a portfolio of businesses whose common denominator may be client base, technology, human expertise or another factor.

A second issue is the breadth of product line. Bankers traditionally have been entranced by the image of being full service, broad line institutions. While this makes eminent sense for a relatively unsophisticated retail or small corporate client, market surveys indicate that, as sophistication rises, clients are increasingly prepared to pick a banking institution on the basis of perceived expertise in specific product markets.

The product line dilemma is particularly painful in the global investment banking business, a sector populated by a number of powerful commercial and investment banks with capital strength, a national client base and a variable claim to product expertise. Imbued with the image of global, interlocking markets, these institutions are determined to offer a global array of products in the Golden Triangle of London, New York and Tokyo despite the high costs involved as well as the acknowledged difficulty of displacing local firms in national securities markets. It is difficult to avoid the conclusion that there will be significant attrition among the 40-odd banking institutions committed in the late 1980s to such a global presence.

A related product line issue is that of the need for vertical integration in the corporate finance sector – one which exercises the management of S.G. Warburg and its UK peers. Does a securities firm with a strong corporate finance/merger and acquisition capability need a sales and distribution function to survive and generate a satisfactory return? In logic, the answer is positive, yet in the competitive marketplace the rewards of adding such an expensive complement do not appear to justify the added expense.

Another issue confronted by both investment and commercial banks is relative cost. The former are exercised by the high cost of maintaining a competitive product line in the face of variable and uncertain demand – whether demand for transactions or appetite for a product which may be superseded by that of a competitor. Commercial banks, on the other hand, are more than conscious of the high and growing cost of their distribution infrastructure. In country after country, they acquiesce in external criticism of networks with too many branches, too many staff per branch and an inefficient use of existing branch personnel.

Yet the bankologist on their behalf takes some comfort in the universally acknowledged impossibility of comparing costs on a bank-to-bank basis. There seems to be no basis for declaring a bank uncompetitive on a cost basis on the grounds of physical size or other measurable trait. As for the threat of a cheaper non-bank competitor, purveyors of credit card and other products delivered without the crushing cost of a bank distribution network can clearly compete in individual product segments, yet the retail banking distribution network still constitutes a unique delivery capability for a broad range of products. An interesting perspective on this dilemma is provided by the experience of two excellent US banks, PNC and First Wachovia, in attempting to achieve merger economies through interstate acquisitions. Both indicated that such economies were largely illusory, at least in the intermediate term, because of the need to invest in new systems and maintain morale and a sense of cultural identity at the human level.

Another management issue brought to the fore by environmental change is whether to integrate different functions serving the same customer base. European and Asian excellent banks like HongkongBank and Deutsche Bank have an understandable desire to separate, both from an organizational and compensation standpoint, product specialists in securities-related businesses from the traditional relationship officers. Yet the experience of the three US money center institutions – and also their other North American peers – is that it is terribly difficult to inculcate a sense of shared values or collaborative effort without a team or partnership approach.

And this approach in itself, as the previous quotations from senior bankers at Citicorp, Bankers Trust and Toronto Dominion have made clear, is virtually impossible to achieve unless each team member feels he is receiving a fair shake in compensation terms. One of the lessons of this volume is that money talks – eventually – in any language or culture. If a global meritocracy is truly the goal of the excellent banks with international ambitions, it is highly unlikely that they can attract and retain superior people without confronting the compensation dilemma which has preoccupied the North American excellent banks.

The last issue to be addressed in this book is the future profile of banking world-wide as measured by the number of separate banking institutions. Put briefly, will massive and apparently unrelieved overcapacity in virtually every banking segment and national market produce an equivalent shrinkage in the number of banks?

Making such predictions has been a favorite indoor sport of both bankers and bankologists each time deregulation or another external force shakes the status quo. The 14,000 banks in the US are the perennial butt of cocktail conversation; how can this situation possibly endure given interstate banking, rising costs, declining margins and the rest? The same goes for national markets elsewhere. Bankologists shake their collective heads at the roughly 1000 banking institutions in countries such as France and Spain. There is no market, apparently, which is not groaning from overcapacity.

A parallel issue is the instinct of both bankers and bank-watchers to fit banks into categories – global, superregional, community and the like – usually on the basis of size or other physical measure. Having established such peer groupings – a well-accepted tenet of bank analysis – the next step is traditionally to declare that one peer group or another is on the way out. In the US interstate banking environment, for example, the middle sized regional is usually judged the victim by presumably falling between the 'rock' of smaller banks with better service capability and the 'hard place' of larger ones with economies of scale.

If there is any single lesson from the interviews in this book, however, it is that aggregate size in itself ranks well towards the bottom of criteria for success among the excellent bankers. Achieving critical mass in one or more businesses, retaining superior people, managing change successfully and maintaining competitive positioning are what count. A superregional in Europe or the US may operate successfully outside its original marketplace, but it faces the same generic challenges as does the so-called global bank such as Citicorp. Everyone acknowledges that economies of scale do exist, but quantifying any conclusions from this statement of presumed fact is beyond the wit of most excellent bankers. Perhaps a typical comment is that of Charles Thayer of PNC, who has personally been on both sides of the negotiating table in the interstate banking wars:

There is clearly a critical mass within a business that permits you to be an efficient provider of services in

that market. I don't know how you measure it; you know when you're there and when you're not there. It's kind of a never-never land. I find it intriguing that a well managed, $100 million bank, which can buy all the systems it needs, can turn in some of the best ROAs and ROEs in the industry. Management makes the difference.

Will there be the massive concentration and amalgamation in various banking markets that has so often been predicted on the basis of economic logic? The answer, in my view, is probably not – except over a very long period of time. True, in that crucible of banking amalgamation in the US called interstate banking, mergers in given market areas have increased concentration. Merger economics in a highly sophisticated investment community have played a major role: selling stockholders have been offered deals they could not refuse, while acquirors have hoped to claw back any dilution by economies and higher volumes. Yet the dynamic profusion of community banks continues to maintain the overall numbers of US banks – witness to the value added by quality service at the retail level.

Outside the US, the outlook for concentration is cloudier. In a Europe gearing up for a single financial space, countless bankers and bankologists have pored over the possibilities. They are limited. True cross border mergers involve cultural leaps of faith which are not popular. The relative absence of stockholder-owned banks and sophisticated financial markets limits the possibility of a US – type drive to 'maximize shareholder value'. Mergers within national or regional boundaries, fostered by regulatory authorities or common ties such as exist in the savings or cooperative sector, are much more likely. The classic case study of regulatory intervention in the late 1980s has been Spain. Having presided over the effective liquidation of half of the Spanish banking community in the early 1980s following massive credit losses, in 1988 the Bank of Spain promoted at least one merger among the top seven remaining institutions to strengthen the system in anticipation of EEC liberalization in 1992.

The regulatory clout in countries like Japan is overwhelming and leads to the conclusion that the process will be a managed one in most countries with stragglers being absorbed without, however, any sharp reduction in the number of players.

There is another, less tangible, barrier to consolidation in banking. David Cates, a leading bank consultant in NY, terms it the 'economic ideology' of banking. Simply stated, it is the widely held belief among bankers – sustained in more substantive terms by their role as repository for a nation's savings – that banking is different   a special enclave set apart from the hurly-burly of commerce and managed by a certain type of responsible executives.

This institutional dignity reacts sharply to unfriendly take-over attempts – witness the year-long struggle by Irving Trust in NY to resist the powerful economic logic of Bank of New York's bid in 1988, and the successful resistance earlier in the decade by Royal Bank of Scotland to the offer by HongkongBank. According to this ideology, chocolate and chemical manufacturers can be bought and sold on their economic merits, but not banks. However justified this logic may be, it is difficult – particularly outside the US – to foresee many unfriendly banking mergers.

There are clearly, however, forces that will drive concentration in particular markets. Asset quality is one. Whatever the rate of external change, banks still usually disappear for the same old reason – not getting the risk dimension right in a business which by definition is highly leveraged. So-called secondary banks in the UK in the 1970s, Texas Savings and Loan Associations in the 1980s, Arab banks lending to private sector clients in the Gulf, consortium banks lending to LDC's in the 1970s – quite apart from the handful of major international banks hit dangerously close to the waterline by LDC lending – are cases in point. Whatever risk disaster overtakes the banks in the 1990s will take its toll of the players in that game.

Stockholder pressure is another. Banks with common ownership ties or traditions are particularly likely to coalesce under competitive pressure. Examples in the 1980s include savings banks in the UK, Spain and Italy as well as their regional entities in Germany, the Landesbanken. The same holds true for co-operative organizations such as the Credit Agricole in France.

What about stockholder economics as a force for concentration? Interstate banking in the US, a market where 'maximizing stockholder value' has become a science, is a laboratory case in point. In a typical US acquisition, the bidder has offered a sufficient premium over book and market value to convince the target's stockholders – and, more reluctantly, management – that selling out made sense. The resulting premium arguably made less sense to acquirors faced with writing off goodwill and justifying an earnings yield (current earnings as a fraction of the purchase cost) on the purchase of 5-10 per cent – generally about half of their own ROE before the purchase. From the comments of the excellent superregionals interviewed in this book plus US bank stock analysts, the purchase economics in most cases are not overwhelming. While these economics may change, the appetite for a massive wave of deals in the US seems to have abated in the late 1980s.

In markets like Japan and Europe, considerations such as national interest, market positioning and the presence of non-stockholder-owned institutions will play a more vital role than that of stockholder value. The views of the Bank of Italy, the Bank of England, the Ministry of Finance in Tokyo and their regulatory peers will, in our view, be the decisive factor in the concentration process in the 1990s.

At this point in our analysis it is appropriate to turn to the issue of how bank equities are valued in the marketplace. If one fundamental strategic option is expansion by acquisition, the price paid for that acquisition and its impact on the buyer's own market valuation are essential ingredients in the strategic recipe. As discussed earlier in this book, the history of interstate banking in the US is largely that of deals taking place when a buyer was prepared to pay a premium over market for a target and recovering any potential dilution of earnings per share – of central importance to American investors – over a reasonable period of time.

To place this analysis in a global context, Tables 10.1 and 10.2 have been prepared to provide performance and valuation data for a sample of major banks in 10 major national banking markets: the US, Canada, UK, Japan, France, Italy, Spain, Germany, Switzerland and Australia. For the performance table in 10.1, after tax return on equity has been used as the best approximation of performance on shareholders funds. The ROE data have generally been taken from IBCA Banking Analysis calculations for a sample of major banks in the given country.

Supplementing this performance index are data from Salomon Brothers publications on the compound annual growth of operating profits – defined to provide some transnational comparability by excluding non-operating items – and earnings per share between 1983 and 1988.

To provide a common standard of performance comparison between countries, the samples' return on equity has been contrasted with both the relevant national consumer price index as employed by IBCA as well as the relevant national long term government bond index. The latter, in our view, provides the best measure of a riskless local currency return to investors against which any local equity investment should be ranked. This relevance is enhanced in the case of the banking sector, as most of the banks in the national samples are regarded at least as quasi-sovereign risks in that their depositors in most cases would be rescued by the central authorities in the event of trouble.

What conclusions can be drawn from the data on performance in Table 10.1? There is a wide range in absolute terms of returns on equity. Of greater significance for comparative purposes is the extent to which ROE exceeds local measures of inflation and risk free return. Here the performance patterns are most instructive.

Firstly, there has been a broad-based improvement in relative performance over the 1983-8 span. From a modest 1.1% spread in 1983, the average ROE (for the six bank composites reporting complete 1988 data) jumped to 7.5% over the average long-term government bond yield. This impressive performance was led by the US, Canadian, UK, Japanese and Spanish banks which each topped their respective risk-free index by at least 7% in 1988. Only in Italy and France have the bank composites had problems in meeting this hurdle.

The leading banks have had somewhat more difficulty in extending this superior performance through to the level of earnings per share growth. Only in Canada, the UK, Japan and Spain have the bank composites both exceeded the local risk-free return and generated a double digit

TABLE 10.1 Selected banking markets: bank performance measures, 1983–88

Country/date	Bank return on equity[1] [1]	Rise in national consumer price index[1] [2]	Net return (1–2)	Long term national government bond yield at year end[2] [3]	Net return (1–3)	Compound annual growth in[3] Operating profit 1983–7	1983–8	Earnings per share 1983–7	1983–8
Canada									
1984	12.9%	3.4%	9.5%	11.7%	1.2%	Neg	21.4	5.6%	15.4%
1987	(5.1)	4.3	(9.4)	10.0	(15.1)				
1988	17.2	NA	NA	10.2	7.0				
United Kingdom									
1984	10.0	4.6	5.4	10.3	(0.3)	Neg	21.2	Neg	12.2
1987	2.2	3.7	(1.5)	9.5	(7.3)				
1988	18.7	NA	NA	9.4	9.3				
United States									
1984	12.2	4.0	8.2	11.6	0.6	Neg	19.4	2.0	6.5
1987	(15.5)	4.4	(19.9)	9.0	(24.5)				
1988	21.6	NA	NA	9.0	12.6				
Japan									
1984	10.4	1.6	8.8	6.3	4.1	10.8	NA	19.6	NA
1987	12.1	1.0	11.2	4.9	7.3				
1988	NA	NA	NA	4.9	NA				
Switzerland									
1984	7.7	2.1	5.6	4.6	3.1	11.2	9.6	8.6	5.4
1987	7.3	1.9	5.4	4.0	3.3				
1988	8.0	NA	NA	4.1	3.9				

Country	Year	(1)	(2)	(3)	(4)	(5)	(6)	(7)	(8)	(9)
West Germany	1984	8.7	2.0	6.7	7.2	1.5	(2.6)	NA	5.1	NA
	1987	7.0	1.0	6.0	6.5	0.5				
	1988	NA	NA	NA	6.6	NA				
Spain	1984	14.2	9.0	5.2	13.9	0.3	NA	NA	21.6	NA
	1987	19.1	4.6	14.5	13.4	5.7				
	1988	22.9	NA	NA	12.8	10.1				
France	1984	8.0	6.7	1.3	12.7	(4.7)	24.7	NA	17.1	NA
	1987	7.5	3.1	4.4	10.0	(2.5)				
	1988	NA	NA	NA	8.5	NA				
Italy	1984	14.3	9.4	4.9	14.5	(0.2)	15.3	NA	18.6	NA
	1987	9.9	5.2	4.7	10.5	(0.6)				
	1988	NA	NA	NA	10.7	NA				
Australia	1984	18.6	NA	NA	13.5	5.1	23.4	25.9	7.5	8.6
	1987	12.6	NA	NA	12.9	(0.3)				
	1988	15.3	NA	NA	13.0	2.3				
Average	1984	11.7	4.8	6.2	10.6	1.1				
	1987	5.7	3.2	1.7	9.1	(3.4)				
	1988[4]	17.3	NA	NA	9.8	7.5				

Notes:

1 *Source:* IBCA Banking Analysis and Salomon Brothers Inc. Based on average of leading national banking institutions for Salomon Brothers Composites.

2 Morgan Guaranty Trust: World Financial Markets.

3 IBCA Banking Analysis and Salomon Brothers Inc. Based on average of major quoted banking institutions in each country.

4 Includes only 6 out of 10 countries whose banks have reported at the time of publication.

– at least 10% – annual compound growth in earnings per share for the 1983-8 period. On the other hand, the French and Italian bank have shown impressive absolute earnings increments from a low base in 1983.

This relatively impressive performance in terms of relative and absolute earnings does not appear to merit the vast fund of investor pessimism for bank stocks. In many national markets, investors' judgements on bank equities range from apathy to deep despair. Overcapacity, unimpressive management, a poor risk/reward ratio and the burden of LDC debt are frequently cited to substantiate these negative views. While these are legitimate concerns, the statistical evidence of Table 10.1 does indicate that major banks in a wide range of countries have managed to produce creditable returns on equity and earnings growth.

Any final conclusions on bank performance must be muted by the obvious problems of transnational data comparability, different valuation standards and choice of banks in the sample. Reported earnings in Germany and Switzerland have much less analytical value than those in Anglo-Saxon countries, while the choice of base rates inevitably shows some banks in a different light than others.

Table 10.2 analyzes valuation parameters for the ten national markets under scrutiny. It incorporates data on the two standard benchmarks which are used throughout the world to evaluate bank stocks: the ratio of price to book value and the price/earnings ratio. In the author's experience, national markets throughout the world use some combination of these two variables as the basis for setting valuation parameters in the respective markets.

The price/earnings multiple is an Anglo-Saxon phenomenon to which investors in many other countries pay only lip service – often for good reason given the ability to conceal true earnings in these markets. Yet it is used on a transnational basis by most global investors. More importantly, within a given market, relative price earnings multiples for different sectors give some indication of investor preference.

For the banking sector, however, by far the most appropriate barometer is book value. Banks – at least those largely dependent on a book of earning assets for generating revenue – are characteristically evaluated as a package of

TABLE 10.2   Valuation parameters: bank stock v. general averages at end-December 1988

Country	Dividend yields			Price/earnings multiple[3]			Price/adjusted book value At year-end 1988[4]
	Bank Stocks[2]	General Index[1]	Bank stocks ÷ General index	Bank stocks[2]	General Index[1]	Bank stocks ÷ General index	
UNITED KINGDOM	5.8%	5.0%	1.16	5.2	10.4	0.50	150%
UNITED STATES (MONEY CENTER)	5.9	3.7	1.59	5.0	11.6	0.43	174
JAPAN	0.23	0.5	0.46	61.4	53.8	1.14	295
GERMANY	3.0	3.6	0.83	18.9	15.6	1.21	171
SWITZERLAND	3.9	2.3	1.70	17.2	14.9	1.15	155
FRANCE	2.6	2.8	0.93	10.4	12.6	0.83	197
ITALY	3.7	2.6	1.42	10.0	15.1	0.66	164
AUSTRALIA	5.9	4.9	1.20	7.0	10.9	0.64	114
SPAIN	2.6	4.0	0.65	13.5	15.6	0.87	304
CANADA	5.4	3.4	1.59	6.9	11.2	0.62	137

Notes:
1 Source: Morgan Stanley Capital Internationl.
2 Solomon Brothers National Bank Composites
3 Price at year-end 1988 dividend by 1988 earnings (actual or estimated)
4 Adjusted to allow for
   100% write-off (after tax) of all unamortized LDC loans, and
   realization (after tax) of excess of disclosed equity holdings over book value.

these assets which, if necessary, can be liquidated over time for a cash flow which is hopefully close to the book value of those assets. In the real world, two types of adjustments must be made to these book values. Some assets – in recent years primarily exposure to LDC nations which are arguably valued above their liquidation value – must be written down to reflect true values. Secondly, undervalued or undisclosed assets should be written up to realisable value. Such 'hidden assets' in reality for the countries under review consist largely of holdings of quoted equities by banks in Japan, Germany, France and Spain which bulk large in balance sheet terms. In sum, any acquiror of banking assets – whether predator or merger partner – should therefore be prepared to pay a price based on such an adjusted book value.

The data in Table 10.2 essentially confirm this simple logic. The sample of banks in the US (the money center institutions), Canada and the UK contain many which value their substantial LDC commitments well above prices which investors regard as reasonable levels, and as a result prices have discounted stated book values ever since the LDC crisis burst upon the world in the early 1980s. At the opposite extreme, the Japanese bank sample sells at a mighty eight times stated book value – in large part because the typical City bank has a portfolio of quoted equities whose excess of market over book value represents three or four times stated book value. Swiss, German and Spanish banks benefit to a lesser extent from such a perception of hidden values.

Each of these distortions can be adjusted by arbitrary up and down valuations which make key – and disputable – assumptions about the true value of LDC loans and the net return after tax which might be realized if the equity holdings were liquidated. What emerges from such adjustments is a remarkably consistent profile of an industry valued essentially on perceived book value which is adjusted upward to allow for truly superior earnings performance and return on investors' funds.

The quoted banking universe seems to be polarized. On the one hand, there is a large group composed of US money center, Canadian and British clearing banks with relatively heavy net LDC exposures. Despite yields on investors' funds which significantly exceed the long term local risk free bond yield, many of these banks sell at a discount to stated book value and at an earnings multiple significantly below the national average. Yet if these asset values are adjusted as described above, the price/adjusted book ratios rise well above 100%. Thus, at year-end 1988, the bank multiples for these three countries represented only 0.43%, 0.62% and 0.50% of the general index for their respective markets. And along with the Australian banks, which also sell at a massive discount to local price/earnings ratios, they command the lowest premia over adjusted book values.

At the other pole are banks without the incubus of major net LDC debt exposure but with strong relative earnings performance, which sell at earnings multiples equal or superior to their local averages as well as a healthy premium over book value. Thus the Swiss, Japanese and German banks boast a premium p/e multiple, while the Spanish banks trail their national average only slightly. Despite their relatively modest profit performance in recent years, the German and Swiss banks command a premium valuation – a tribute to their economic power as viewed by local investors.

What strategic conclusions can be drawn from this brief overview of bank stock pricing on a global scale? Firstly, that there is a consistent valuation pattern which is relevant for the leading bank stock markets. Secondly, that banks which perform in a superior fashion generally do obtain superior valuation ratios. And thirdly, that the resulting valuation parameters vary widely in absolute terms and offer considerable theoretical opportunities for amalgamations which would benefit the stockholders of both the buyer and the seller.

As an example, Swiss and German banks armed with high price/earnings multiples but with relative low apparent yields on equity would appear a perfect match for some British banks with precisely the reverse posture. The match is improved by the formers' modest LDC exposure which would theoretically permit them to absorb the British banks' overseas commitments without strain. Within a given country such as Spain, there are wide variances in multiples; at year-end 1988 Banco Santander sold at a p/e multiple twice that of Banco Popular despite roughly equivalent earnings performance over the years.

But the grand daddy of all possible combinations is the possible role to be played by Japanese banks. With seven of the top ten (as measured, traditionally, in asset size) banks in the world now based in Osaka or Tokyo rather than NY or London – and all ten as measured by market capitalization – the Japanese possess the absolute size to digest their overseas peers with minimal effort. If to this absolute clout is added the lofty price/earnings multiples at which Japanese banks have sold in the latter portion of the 1980s, the economics of consolidation become compelling. When to this heady recipe is finally stirred in the competitive analogy of Japanese product superiority in the automotive and electronics business, the possibilities of Japanese domination become mind-boggling.

Yet even the most imaginative bankologist can detect few signs of this colossus realizing its full potential. The principal reason was articulated earlier in this volume: the universally-acknowledged need to be able to manage diversity – and particularly local businesses outside one's natural franchise. Japanese banks have recognized this cultural difficulty by eschewing overseas expension in the retail/small corporate sector – with the sole exception of the California market, in which they collectively are a significant but hardly very profitable player in contrast to the leaders such as Wells Fargo. This self-imposed embargo may well be lifted in the 1990s, as the Japanese gain confidence in their ability to run a true global meritocracy. But for the moment their international thrust is based on low yielding, traditional products and the acquisition of the skills needed to build a capability in the newer, higher value-added ones such as rate risk management and corporate finance. Their strategic focus – particularly following the imposition of standard capital adequacy rules – is increasingly on their Japanese client base. The 1990s may bring a more ambitious thrust, but for the moment the threat is a distant one.

The cultural barriers blocking Japanese domination of the world's national banking markets are echoed in different accents in many other markets. In the context of European integration in 1992, for example, as we have seen in earlier chapters, the statistical arguments for cross border acquisitions pale before the challenge of managing different cultures and possibly alienating key constituencies in the acquired bank's market.

In sum, the outlook for the short and intermediate term is for continued overcapacity with the winners successfully differentiating themselves and achieving competitive advantage in one or more businesses – some of which may be far removed from traditional banking. In reviewing the management issues and critical success factors discussed earlier in this book, one is struck by two thoughts; the virtual unanimity of views on how to manage change, and the growing difficulty of establishing competitive advantage in the overall financial services business.

In *Excellence in Banking,* there was a reasonable difference of opinion on the extent of change to be faced and the responses – structure, compensation, need for specialist skills, etc. – required. Now all the excellent banks acknowledge that they are inextricably linked to the locomotive of change which will draw them into previously uncharted terrain – functional organization structures, across-the-board incentive compensation, new products, managing overseas businesses with local staff, massive technology expenditures just to stay in a given business, and the like.

That is the bad news. The good news is that their excellent peers – in particular the trio of US excellent money center banks – have been there already and can offer a friendly correspondent banking hand guiding them over the rough bits. And, whatever the national market, the guidance follows familiar lines: use compensation to guide cultural change, communicate, go for the best people, don't enter businesses if you're not comfortable with the risk, bring different cultures together on the base of a few shared but relevant values, and so forth.

It is a quite different challenge to confront the outside world and make money. The latter goal has now become gospel throughout the banking world – in Japan as well as Europe, and the final testament of this gospel was the global agreement in 1988 – a landmark in banking regulation – on minimum risk adjusted capital adequacy guidelines. Lip service in some markets has been reinforced by regulatory clout, albeit not by investor pressure in many markets with less than Anglo-Saxon commitment to shareholder values.

The principal challenge thus remains the external market – a business whose overcapacity is unlikely to diminish radically over the careers of today's top managers. Excellent national banks like Deutsche Bank and National Westminster as well as top securities houses like S.G. Warburg will continue to agonize over the attractions of committing resources abroad or domestically. Others with fewer strategic choices, such as the US money center banks, will increasingly become product-oriented institutions like their Wall Street brethren. And the exigencies of achieving critical mass – or rather a leading market share – will drive them progressively away from a broad range of traditional banking products to a differentiated package linked by the factor of competitive advantage rather than any intellectual logic.

John Rudy, head of the international banking practice of Greenwich Associates, sums up the experience of many years of evaluating bank performance from the client's perspective:

In building competitive advantage, the excellent banks have learned to say 'no' to themselves as they narrow their business base and deny expansion for its own sake, and to customers, in refusing to treat with them under unattractive terms of trade. Excellent bank strategic ambition and execution is now practical, circumscribed – and increasingly piercing. It is responsive to market forces, defining a future that is *intensive*, not *extensive*.

11 Banking Excellence Revisited: Winners and Losers in an Environment of Competition and Change

The four critical success factors discussed in Chapters 7-10 should serve as an analytical framework to identify those banking institutions best able to prosper in a dynamic environment of change. Yet there are still nagging doubts in applying them to specific banks – particularly when comparing the panel's list of excellent institutions over the four year period between 1984 and 1988. As was pointed out in Chapter 2, half of the select few in 1984 did not reappear four years later. More specifically, three banks which received over half of the panel's votes for *Excellence in Banking* – Security Pacific, Sumitomo Bank and Swiss Bank Corporation – received only a scattering of votes for this volume.

What lies behind this change in perception? Have the drop-outs lost their patina as excellent institutions? What has happened in the intervening years to change bankologists' perceptions? More important from the author's standpoint, how valid are the conclusions reached in *Excellence in Banking* on the characteristics of excellence and the challenges to be faced by these institutions in the future? The final sentence of *Excellence in Banking*, referring to nine specific challenges, concluded that:

Response to these challenges will separate the excellent banks of the future from the also-rans.

The goal of this final chapter is thus to revisit the conclusions of *Excellence in Banking* in the light of subsequent experience and the analysis of environmental change and critical success factors contained in this volume. To do so, the author has also revisited individual panel members, armed with the analysis of Chapters 1-10 of this book, in search of enlightenment with specific reference to changes in the list of excellent institutions. Our queries are straightforward. Which – if any – of the ten traits of excellence in 1984 have been most relevant in an era of change? How well have excellent banks – both those which fell from grace and those which graced both lists – met the nine challenges described in *Excellence in Banking*? And finally, the last and supreme question: What happens when one applies the four critical factors for success in a changing world to individual excellent institutions?

The starting point for this interrogation is the list of ten characteristics of excellent banks beginning on p. 118 of *Excellence in Banking*. Let's take them in turn, first quoting the characteristic and then commenting on our subsequent findings.

11.1   AN OPEN CULTURE

The starting point for excellence is an environment where extensive vertical and horizontal communications take place as a matter of course ... It would seem that an open culture is essential to sound and effective decision making, to the communication system which unites a large and complex organization, and to the healthy resolution of the inevitable conflicts which arise in the allocation of scarce resources.

All the evidence of the past few years confirms the validity of this trait. The newcomers to the excellent ranks such as S.G. Warburg and Credit Suisse/CSFB bear witness to the virtues of solid communication – even over-communication.

Warburg's famed insistence on internal memo-writing and exchange of correspondence and the months of dialogue which preceded the restructuring of First Boston and Credit Suisse First Boston in 1988 add to the collection of war stories of intensive communication among excellent banks. The rapid expansion of functional, product-based structures – usually on a global basis – demands such communication. In a strategic sense, as Tom Frost of National Westminster Bank has pointed out, getting all the troops in a 55,000-strong organization to face in one direction requires more than a simple memo to all hands from the chief executive.

As circumstances change, the demands on the open culture evolve. Morgan's Bruce Brackenridge's graphic description of the need for lateral, rather than vertical, communication in a global, product-oriented structure is a case in point. Partnership between buy and sell side staffers is essential in a bank like Toronto Dominion determined both to maintain a single culture yet successfully enter the investment banking arena. As Willie Purves of Hongkong Bank has emphasized, the conflicts and overlaps of the stockbrokerage and commercial banking cultures must be addressed and dealt with openly by the chief executive. And Bankers Trust and National Westminster Bank are among the latest to discover that, at least with a common client base, the communication barriers between investment and commercial bankers must eventually be broken down to ensure an effective response to client needs.

The drawbacks to an open culture have also been revealed by the evidence of the past four years. Deutsche Bank's long deliberations over strategy and structure – as well as specific issues such as entry into the insurance sector – confirm the vast amount of time needed for achieving the consensus required to change the course of the ship of state. The level of conflict in institutions such as National Westminster, J.P. Morgan and Citicorp has clearly risen as the challenges of the securities-related products are met.

Yet our conclusions are the same: the excellent banking institutions have found no better means of running their businesses. The open culture remains a prime trait of excellence.

11.2   STRONG SHARED VALUES

Within the context of this open culture, the unifying element is a strong sense of shared values throughout the managerial ranks of the organization ... The principal means of developing such values is the excellent banks' almost universal practice of growing their own talent. This has obvious potential drawbacks, both in promoting parochial thinking today and adapting to new competitive conditions tomorrow.

Experience in the latter half of the 1980s has confirmed the relevance of shared cultural values. Among the banks featuring in both volumes, First Wachovia's top managers have emphasized the importance, as Bud Baker puts it, of returning in turbulent times to the pole star of basic values. HongkongBank clings tenaciously to its doctrine of federalism despite the temptation to merge its capital market units, while Citicorp continues to espouse the virtues of decentralization and diversity. Among the newcomers to the list, S.G. Warburg has been able to extend the Warburg values of strong internal communication and commitment to providing independent advice to the merged institution.

The stresses of change and diversity, however, have highlighted a new dimension of shared values. Confronted with a multiplication of cultures within a single group by virtue of mergers and the recruitment of newcomers, the challenge is to provide a linkage, a common denominator, which brings the disparate groups together. For First Wachovia, it is recourse to the traditional values of conservatism and balance; for Morgan it is understandably the old Morgan virtues of quality – both of product and customer.

The challenge of identifying and propagating such unifying traits is particularly difficult in a large commercial bank whose strength has been an internal cohesion built on lifetime employment, strong loyalties and, in many respects, a rejection of things foreign. This is the challenge, for example, faced by National Westminster as it struggles to build bridges – to quote Tom Frost – between its investment and commercial banking businesses. Among the excellent banks, the contrast between this dilemma and, for example, the relative success of NatWest's City neighbor, S.G. Warburg, is striking. Across the Atlantic, PNC's solution to diversity is to promote and bring together the top officers of its merged entities.

11.3   PROFIT PERFORMANCE AS A VALUE

The distinction between numbers-driven and value-driven is not a fundamental one for most banks. For them explicitly or implicitly, it is the bottom line that constitutes the relevant value ... What drives the great majority of excellent banks is a satisfactory earnings trend.

This distinction, which was central for the authors of *In Search of Excellence*, produced some ambiguous responses in 1984. In retrospect, much of this apparent ambiguity reflected the different stages of the evolutionary life cycle on which banks find themselves. For national banks benefitting from relatively sheltered and lucrative home markets – or, in the case of the Japanese institutions which danced to a Ministry of Finance tune – focus on profitability could be regarded as an irritation which was more the province of the American banks with their legendary preoccupation with quarterly profits.

This irritation has now become a strategic priority – in part at least because of the 1988 agreement in the Cooke Committee of the Bank for International Settlements on risk weightings and the need to maintain global capital standards. As banks have done their planning sums in the light of these guidelines, product and customer profitability have assumed a new importance.

Yet the experience of the past four years for other banks on the competitive life cycle has shown the limits of reliance on bottom line results. For banks like Bankers Trust and Citicorp, there is a new understanding of what Messrs Waterman and Peters had in mind in focussing on non-financial values. High performers – particularly those recruited from the marketplace on an incentive basis - have understandably left no stone unturned in their efforts to maximize their particular profit center contribution. The damage done to efforts to build bridges to the more pedestrian functions of the organization is reflected in the author's interview notes – whose pungent comments on incentive compensation rarely survived the editors' red pencil.

In sum, profit performance is truly a driving force for the excellent banks, yet the issue for an increasing number is one of balance between the bottom line and non-financial values. Thus virtues such as federalism for HongkongBank, decentralization for Citicorp and independent advice for Warburg not only provide essential cultural linkages but also hopefully produce incremental profits by setting the bank apart from its rivals.

11.4   A CUSTOMER-DRIVEN ORIENTATION

In common with the excellent companies described in *In Search of Excellence*, the excellent banks have generally oriented themselves around their customers. Perhaps a bit later than non-banks, they have segmented their markets, restructured their organizations and delivery systems to deal with the needs of particular segments, gone out to the customer to determine his needs and developed products and people skills accordingly.

A tidal wave of measures to bring bankers closer to their customers has characterized the period since *Excellence in Banking* was written – among excellent as well as a broad range of other institutions. Segmentation of the delivery system has become a byword as banks – particularly those with vast branch networks – are attempting, like National Westminster, to reverse the proportion of selling to back office personnel. As Charles Thayer of PNC pointed out, error rates are costly both in terms of expense and lost good will, and the relative profitability of unsophisticated retail and small corporate customers has unleashed a reconfiguration of branch systems, sales training of branch staff and investment in electronic delivery systems by banks such as PNC, National Westminster and Toronto Dominion.

In the corporate or wholesale sector, the trend has been towards a functional or product structure in banks like Warburg and Morgan to bring the latest product innovations closer to the customer. Thus swaps, M and A and foreign exchange are now global products managed centrally with key personnel scattered throughout the world.

Moving closer to the customer – even the unglamorous yet highly profitable retail client – is thus a characteristic of excellent banks. Yet, as in several other qualities we are analyzing, it is also a trait – or at least goal – of virtually every banking institution in the world.

11.5 WILLINGNESS TO INVEST IN NEW PRODUCTS

Drawing conclusions on innovation is hazardous given the uncertainties of the economic merit of new banking products and the conflict over whether being first provides a lasting competitive advantage. Yet it is quite clear that the vast majority of well-managed banks is prepared to invest considerable funds and management time when management is convinced of the merits of the project.

It is in new product development that the bankologist glimpses increased differentiation and focus among the banking community. For most excellent banks, the cost of new product investment and the risk of failure still argue for caution and imitation of the pioneer investor. Veteran excellent chief executives like John Medlin and Dick Thomson prefer,to quote the former, to be on the leading, not bleeding, edge of new product development. Thus leaders like National Westminster Bank, Union Bank of Switzerland and Deutsche Bank are only now installing the information technology and building expertise in rate risk management products which some of their American peers introduced several years earlier.

For banks such as the US money center triad of J.P. Morgan, Bankers Trust and Citicorp, product investment – particularly in these two domains of information technology and rate risk management products such as swaps and options – is a matter of competitive survival. The outsider senses that the gap between leaders and followers in these key sectors has widened considerably since *Excellence in Banking* was written. Information technology and revenue-generating products such as swaps and options are obviously linked; these arbitrage products can add value only with a highly sophisticated, real-time analysis of rates taken from a variety of markets. The gains to pioneers like Bankers Trust have been significant in terms of supporting a highly profitable foreign exchange and securities issuance activity. The costs are equally terrifying both in terms of absolute investment as well as of rapid product obsolescence.

In another dimension of information technology, that of data processing in more mundane products such as cash management, one is aware of a handful of leaders distancing themselves from the pack. First Wachovia is thus joining a select group of US banks such as Banc One and State Street Bank which have a technological edge in the processing of vast amounts of data.

To summarize, competitive pressures in the late 1980s have forced a limited number of banking institutions to differentiate themselves in the product arena from the great mass of banks offering a standard range of financial products to traditional customers. The banking world is still far from the R and D budgets typical of a pharmaceutical or engineering company, but the trend is clear.

11.6   STRONG AND CONSISTENT LEADERSHIP

Of all the characteristics of banking excellence, it is leadership which separates the sheep from the goats. Countless banks perform well in so many respects yet do not provide a consistent game plan enforced consistently and effectively by the top management team. The excellent banks do, and they do it without necessarily having a grand strategic scheme.

The research for this book has pointed to two conclusions on the subject of leadership. First, the burden of leadership is even heavier in times of change such as the present. One has but to focus on the essential role played by Charlie Sanford in Bankers Trust's merchant banking strategy, that of John Medlin in the merger process with First Atlanta, that of Sir David Scholey in S.G. Warburg's four way merger and that of Willie Purves in enforcing a federalist doctrine for HongkongBank. Without the ceaseless and active intervention of these key individuals, the process of change would have assumed a totally different shape.

The challenge for the future is equally clear for banks addressing the issue of managing diversity. Union Bank of Switzerland is unlikely to succeed in truly decentralizing its international business without strong and active leadership which manages this delicate process, while the same can be said for National Westminster as it knits together its investment and commercial banking arms.

Secondly, the presence of a grand strategic scheme has become far more relevant in today's era of violent change. Without such a road map supported by strong leadership, getting the troops to face in one direction is virtually impossible. One can acknowledge the truth of George Vojta's point in *Excellence in Banking* that strategy comes from the minds of people rather than a paper document, but the need to make the kind of strategic choices over which excellent banks like Toronto Dominion, Deutsche Bank and J.P. Morgan are agonizing demands reaching some form of consensus which is recorded in some form of road map. Once the kind of vision described by Tom Frost becomes a consensus, management can focus on implementation – but not before.

Excellence in Banking also focussed on the problem of continuity of leadership. Most of the chief executives interviewed for this volume were still in place four years later, shepherding the flock in the same strategic direction. In others, however, a change in leadership has often meant a perceptible change in direction as well as style. At one extreme is the handover at Bankers Trust, where Charlie Sanford has carried on the strategy initiated under Al Brittain. At Ciricorp, John Reed's background in retail banking and information technology – coupled with the massive profit contribution of the retail function – have, in the minds of many of his colleagues, produced a different tilt to the bank's strategy. Perhaps the most marked change is at Deutsche Bank, where Dr Alfred Herrhausen's assumption of the reins of leadership has propelled the bank in the direction of a diversified product base as well as greater focus on international expansion.

One of the interesting developments between 1984 and 1988 has been evidence of a movement in some excellent banks away from the leadership extreme of pure democracy toward the middle ground of a single leader supported by a strong management team. Perhaps the most extreme case is that of Swiss Bank Corporation, which replaced its federalist management committee with a rotating head by a chief executive. Deutsche Bank also moved from leadership provided by two speakers of the Board to a single chief executive. Arguably the pressure for crisper decision making lies behind this apparent trend.

To sum up, a changing environment reinforces the differentiating role played by leadership and strategy. Finding the right balance between change and stability, entrepreneurship and conservatism, and democracy and dictatorship must be one of the most difficult tasks for bank management confronting the 1990s.

11.7   COMMITMENT TO RECRUIT THE BEST

For the excellent banks committed to growing their own, the recruitment process is the keystone for investment in human resources ... The focus for most excellent banks will be a combination of intelligence, ability to work as a team player, adaptiveness and commitment ... The need for new skills plus the need to select out sub-par performers will have their impact on the educational as well as skills level required.

The interview process for this book not only confirmed the central importance of this trait but also pointed up some of the challenges confronting management once these skills have been acquired. One consequence has been the sharp conflict between the profit motivation of highly incentivized revenue-generators and the perceived broader interests of the bank as a whole. Most of the excellent banks have overcome their reservations about incentive compensation, but the management time commitment and the inherent messiness of the reward process in banks like S.G. Warburg, J.P. Morgan and Bankers Trust constitute a major source of concern.

Equally central are the problems posed by diversity. The recruitment of specialists without a lifetime career commitment to their employer poses a major challenge to Citicorp and others broadening their product reach. Integration in the geographic sense is of crucial importance to banks like Union Bank of Switzerland and Deutsche Bank, who acknowledge that their ability to penetrate overseas markets is a function of their success in attracting and motivating superior local talent.

Finally, the process of integrating high performance outsiders into a traditional banking structure obliges banks to review their decision making as well as organizational structures. The young management trainees interviewed made it clear that they had little time for turf fights, a prolonged decision making process, or barriers to communicating laterally.

Ranking the quality of people as one of the four key success factors in today's banking environment is hardly a surprising conclusion. Actually achieving such a goal will, in our view, constitute one of the toughest challenges for even the very best of our sample.

11.8 INVESTMENT IN TRAINING AND CAREER DEVELOPMENT

A corollary excellent trait to recruitment is a commitment to pour resources, including top management time, into the training and career development of those selected. The likely continuation of inbreeding, the role of training in improving communications, the transformation of banking products, the frequent shortfall in managerial skills, the growing personnel selectivity – all argue for such investment.

Investing in people has indeed become one of the shibboleths of banking throughout the world – to the lasting benefit of a horde of consultants offering product and management development skills training. Branch staff have been taught to recognize the primacy of client needs, relationship managers instructed in the mysteries of rate risk management products and branch managers introduced to the fine art of managing people. Our conversations with excellent bankers indicate that this investment has produced mixed rewards: some students pass with flying colors, others squeak by, while still others cannot be reconstructed and are offered generous early retirement packages. Career development in the excellent banks continues to take the form of strategic postings in staff and line jobs as well as overseas assignments.

Yet despite herculean efforts to recruit and develop the best, the excellent banks continue to lose talent frustrated by perceived bureaucracy, lack of recognition and reward, and more attractive packages offered by the competition. Capital market specialists in particular in J.P. Morgan, Citicorp and National Westminster Bank as well as S.G. Warburg have been lured away.

11.9   A MATRIX-BASED MANAGEMENT INFORMATION SYSTEM

The development of product and client management information is one of the most visible current trends among the excellent banks. Some, like Citibank and Bankers Trust, have already arrived, while others are devoting considerable resources to getting there.

Chapter 4 of this book has elaborated both the challenges and responses of managing technology in the broadest sense. While the outsider – and maybe even the insider – is incapable of measuring both the cost and benefit of the investment in information technology, the end result varies widely even among the world's best managed banking institutions. The nirvana of a global system which measures consolidated rate risk as well as product and customer profitability still eludes many of the excellent banks. The relative shortage of project management skills, the high cost of software investment, the difficulty in agreeing cost allocations – all have led to what

Goerge Vojta of Bankers Trust describes as a patchwork quilt of overlapping, incompatible systems for many banks.

As Tom Frost of National Westminster points out, bank management has the feeling of being on a never-ending roller coaster of investment in information technology. There may be leaders like Citicorp and Bankers Trust and relative laggards like Union Bank of Switzerland at a given point in time, but all are facing the same challenge of keeping up with changing technology, an evolving product range and expanding physical network.

Yet in the last analysis, building an effective management information system – or any other dimension of information technology – calls upon some fairly basic managerial skills: good communication between user and supplier, setting specific project goals and monitoring progress, and obtaining ownership from the user. The bankologist thus arrives at the not very remarkable conclusion that the banks best able to manage technology are those which do a professional job of managing other aspects of their business.

11.10   A STRONG AND BALANCED CREDIT PROCESS

Events of the past decade have confirmed the essential need for a respected and introspective credit process. Credit extension is still a matter of judgement, but errors in execution as well as the need for a 'what if' analysis justify a major investment in this process. Whether pre-or post-approval, the process must establish procedural rules as well as enable top management to balance the enthusiasm of lending advocates.

The experience of the past four years as gleaned from the interview processs not only reinforces this conclusion but also leads one to broaden it to include the twin nemeses preoccupying management in late 1988 – namely leveraged finance and the new rate risk management products. The repeated warnings by excellent bankers in J.P. Morgan, Citicorp, Bankers Trust and others to understand a new swap or option product before setting limits bear witness to the pressures they are under from enthusiastic product specialists to take advantage of exciting perceived profit

opportunities. The same need for balance – this time
in assessing downside risk in highly leveraged borrowers
– is evident in the LBO business.

One may or may not agree with Larry Glenn of Citicorp
that there is basically little new under the sun in these
product areas, but what is certain is that the management dilemma is the same – greed vs. fear. The actual
losses suffered by the excellent banks since the writing
of *Excellence in Banking* have in aggregate been relatively
minor in a historical context: position losses during stock
market breaks such as October 1987, further writedowns
of LDC debt incurred many years earlier, and regional or
industry-specific problems such as Texas or the Arab Gulf.

It is in this context that one can revisit the fall from
grace of Texas Commerce Bank shortly after the interviews for *Excellence in Banking*. This fall substantiated both
the author's acknowledgement that such drop-outs would
be inevitable as well as the affirmation that asset quality
problems account for virtually all bank failures throughout
history. As mentioned in Chapter 1, it is impossible for
the outsider to evaluate whether a different management
strategy would have permitted Texas Commerce to sail
through the state's disastrous economic downturn. Yet what
is fascinating in querying our panel is to be told repeatedly
that TCB, while one of the first major Texas banks to report
earnings problems, has ultimately outperformed its peers in
terms of the low level of actual losses suffered.

In looking to the future, it is clear that the competitive
pressures to assume credit, rate or other risks are strong
and growing. The lesson of the past decade, however, is
that the excellent banks will at least thoroughly debate
the nature and extent of these risks and, as Dr Guth
of Deutsche Bank put it when evaluating interest rate
risk in Germany in the early 1980s or John Medlin of
First Wachovia in agonizing over LBOs, ultimately choose
a conservative point on the risk/reward spectrum.

Given these ten characteristics of the excellent bank,
Excellence in Banking concluded with a list of challenges
for the future. In our search for answers to the evolution of our list of such institutions, it might be useful
to examine this list for useful clues.

Several of these challenges have already been analyzed at length in previous chapters. *More effective cross selling* has been – and continues to be – a problem for banking institutions shaping their branch networks as a product distribution system rather than source of reliable and inexpensive deposits. *Pay for performance*, as we have learned, is the flashpoint of conflict between the traditional culture and the drive for profit maximization.

More outsiders have indeed *been recruited:* the US money center banks in particular have tapped retail marketing specialists, industrial managers for their development capital arms, and others who previously had seen the inside of a bank only as retail depositors. Of equal significance for many excellent European banks has been recruiting foreign nationals at top management level. Thus a German national, Hans-Joerg Rudloff, runs Credit Suisse's international securities function, while a Briton does the same at Swiss Bank Corporation. *Higher eductional standards* are indeed being introduced, particularly in major retail banks, as we have seen at Toronto Dominion Bank and National Westminster Bank, to redress the problem described by Charles Thayer and Urban Joseph of teenagers hired in the postwar years largely because of their low cost.

In the realm of products, the *greater emphasis on noncredit products* has continued apace. Selling information as a product – as advertised by Citicorp and S-E-Banken – has not proven particularly remunerative, but many excellent Anglo-Saxon banks have cleaned up in innovative rate risk management products such as swaps. Data processing specialists like First Wachovia have distanced themselves further from the competition.

In the more traditional capital market products such as securities underwriting and distribution and corporate financial advice, however, the newcomers have come up against fierce competition from the established players, massive overcapacity and a cyclical market in the latter 1980s. In this particular assault, as we shall see below, our panel has separated many perceived winners from losers among our original list of excellent institutions.

Earlier chapters of this volume have graphically described how the *culture* of each of our excellent banks *has been tested* by the break-up of the family feeling and other consequences of the perceived need to raise performance standards. None has been holed below the waterline by this barrage, but the level of conflict is high and rising – particularly in banking institutions like National Westminster and J.P. Morgan committed to penetrating the capital market sector.

One final challenge foreshadowed by *Excellence in Banking* is that of *entrepreneurship and a bias for action*, the two traits of non-bank firms described in *In Search of Excellence* which were notable for their absence in most excellent banks. The evidence accumulated in this book confirms our prediction that entry into the capital markets arena and the focus on bottom line performance have, indeed, brought these qualities to the fore. Listening to the words of Hans-Joerg Rudloff of Credit Suisse First Boston, the acknowledged leader in the global securities business, is sufficient confirmation that each of these qualities is a critical factor for success in the securities business. *Doing Deals*, a thoughtful and incisive book on investment banking in the US by Dwight Crane and Robert Eccles, describes in vivid detail the management practices in this business.

Revisiting the conclusions of *Excellence in Banking* does thus provide some clues as to what might differentiate winners from losers in the choice of excellent banks. But before we attempt our own analysis, it seems imperative that we question again the members of our panel who, after all, made the selection both in 1984 and 1988. In comparing their two lists of excellent banking institutions, what did they have in mind in adding or dropping banks? For each panelist, therefore, our question focused on relative performance in the intervening period and the implications for managerial superiority.

11.11 PENETRATING NEW MARKETS

The first theme of the responses was the weight given to relative success in penetrating major new product and geographic markets. Acknowledging that long term earnings growth for most will be a function of successful entry into new markets, their attention has been focused, for example, on perceived success in entering the investment banking business as well as major national markets outside their home base.

In this context, both Barclays and Swiss Bank Corporation suffered in the view of panel members who dropped them from the 1988 list – despite acknowledging that both continued to be extremely well managed institutions. Barclays was perceived to be less successful than competitors such as S.G. Warburg in its efforts to propel its investment bank, Barclays De Zoete Wedd, into the leadership ranks of London-based global institutions. And its efforts to build a network in the US, culminating in the sale of its California branch network, paled beside the relative success of National Westminster in turning its New York State affiliate around.

Swiss Bank Corporation was universally perceived by virtually all panel members to have retained its position domestically among the leading Swiss banks, yet rival Credit Suisse's dominance of the international investment banking business through Credit Suisse First Boston clearly played a role in switching votes to Credit Suisse. This view was reinforced at the end of 1988 when First Boston in New York was merged into CSFB, thereby making the Swiss parent the only foreign institution to control a major successful investment banking house in the fiercely competitive US market. In contrast, Swiss Bank Corporation's wholly-owned counterpart still operated in the red in 1988 and was perceived by many to be struggling to establish its identity in an overcrowded marketplace.

In terms of pure geographic expansion, a fascinating case in point is Bayerische Vereinsbank in Germany, which garnered a significant number of votes in 1984 but was virtually ignored in 1988 by the panel. No panelist had a bad word for this excellent regional institution, yet most agreed that it had not – by design or failure of effort – succeeded in imposing itself outside its traditional domestic market. Bayerische Vereinsbank thus fell, in the view of many panelists, into the large category of extremely successful regional or national institutions who would thrive – or fall – with their local market but not, as with such excellent counterparts as PNC Financial or HongkongBank, break out of their home base through successful acquisitions or organic growth.

To quote one of our panelists:

> **They are king of a mountain [in Bavaria] which looms large in Germany and are skillful in responding to German needs. That's fine but what's next? Can they successfully merge cultures? The framework has changed.**

Adds another observer of the German scene:

> **Bayerische Vereinsbank haven't done anything significantly wrong. The issue is how to expand internationally without endangering their good record.**

The same point is made by another panelist who dropped Sweden's S-E-Banken from his list in 1988:

> **S-E-Banken is still chugging along; they've stuck to their knitting and are still the best international bank in Scandinavia. But on a world scale others have done better. They had a somewhat grander design of becoming more than a pan-Scandinavian bank; it was grander than they were able to achieve. They've recognized the bounds of the market they're dealing in and are doing very well in their own court.**

11.12 MANAGEMENT EFFECTIVENESS

A second theme articulated by the panel in dropping names from the excellent list is an embarrassing – and therefore well-publicized – setback which raises the issue of effective management controls. Evaluating the true significance of such setbacks is virtually impossible for the outsider, but the attention automatically given to excellent banks' publicized sins ensures the flow of a certain amount of crocodile tears at the bending or loss of a halo.

Such a case in point is the twin setbacks – at least in the short term – experienced by Sumitomo Bank in its investment in Goldman Sachs in New York and acquisition of the Heiwa Sogo bank to bolster its Tokyo branch network. Sumitomo Bank thus fell from a majority selection in 1984 to a scattering of votes in 1988 reflecting the widely perceived embarrassment stemming from Heiwa Sogo asset write-offs and the regulatory limitations imposed on functional collaboration – one of the prime objectives of the 15 per cent investment – between Goldman Sachs and Sumitomo. The premature – by a few months – retirement of the bank's President was mentioned by most panelists as confirming the importance of these blows.

Another embarrassment much quoted by the panelists was Barclays' losses in the mid-1980s on overseas lending in the US, Italy and other foreign markets which pointed in their view to poor management controls. For one Barclays-watcher, these were a symptom of a more serious disease:

There was a lot of faulty execution. It's the evolution from a family-oriented to a professional management which is going on before our eyes. Complacency has been one of the worst problems.

Another embarrassment for an excellent bank has been Swiss Bank Corporation's role in financing the German Coop group, which in late 1988 was developing into a major scandal of mismanagement and insider dealing. Many of our panelists cited this as an example of over-aggressive business development abroad for a bank which had been the leader among Swiss banks in the international commercial banking arena.

The objective outsider attempting to take a long term view must instinctively discount the negative conclusions drawn from such misfortunes which attract the public eye – knowing that far more egregious sins may be concealed in a bank's internal accounts. Yet the point is that excellence, to opinion formers such as our panel, requires a sufficiently high standard of execution to avoid such misdeeds in the far reaches of the network.

11.13 LOSING GROUND TO RIVALS

A third echo reverberating from our panel's comments is the downgrading of a bank clearly overtaken in some major dimension by its rivals. The classic case in point is Bank of Tokyo, which disappeared from the excellent list in 1988. Throughout the postwar era, Bank of Tokyo with its privileged position as Japan's foreign exchange bank has been regarded as a class act – a role model for international expertise and high calibre people. As a semi-official arm of the Ministry of Finance as Japan flexed its international muscles, the bank prospered.

In the mid-1980s, however, the environment uniformly turned sour. As Japan's leading international lender, Bank of Tokyo had accumulated an exposure to developing countries which was a multiple of its peers as well as its capital base. Dollar-denominated earnings from its vast offshore network collapsed with the rising yen. And deregulation in Tokyo meant that its rivals, who unlike Bank of Tokyo benefitted from a profitable domestic network, were free to compete with Bank of Tokyo abroad.

The challenge thus posed was clear to the Bank of Tokyo managers interviewed in 1984. Yet since then it has been rivals such as Industrial Bank of Japan which have garnered superior positions in capital market league tables, led Japanese institutions in new product development and taken the lead in profitably channeling Japanese exports of capital. To quote one of our panelists:

> **They've been somewhat slow to adjust to a different world. They were tops five years ago, but they're no longer the dominant Japanese bank in most respects. IBJ and Sumitomo are more aggressive. Time will tell – they may be coming out it with the acquisition of Union Bank in California.**

Another observer, who is particularly concerned about the LDC debt problem, adds:

> **The role of Japanese banks internationally has evolved, leaving Bank of Tokyo in the dust. The ultimate slap in the face was when the Ministry of Finance did not allow banks to tax-effect their provisions on LDC debts; they don't get any favors even from the MOF. What is their raison d'etre?**

The same focus on momentum – of being overtaken by the competition – is reflected in the choice of National

Westminster in 1988 over Barclays. By the mid-1980s, NatWest had come to dominate the performance ratios beloved of financial analysts as Barclays' asset quality deteriorated and overseas businesses struggled. On the Continent, as we have discussed above, Credit Suisse's successful management of its international investment banking strategy clearly has overshadowed memories of the Chiasso scandal in the late 1970s.

11.14 EFFECTIVENESS OF STRATEGY

A final theme expressed by the panel is their judgement on a bank's strategy. While one can question the ability of an outsider to challenge management's presumably better informed views on how to position itself against its competitors, such judgements are part of the fabric of a bank's external image.

The excellent bank which suffered most between the two polls from this factor is Security Pacific, which gleaned a majority of votes in 1984 from panelists impressed by the vigor of its product and geographic initiatives. Its subsequent marked drop in esteem stems from a widespread concern that Security Pacific has not only spread itself too thin in terms of critical mass but has also encountered earnings problems in some of its more aggressive ventures. The acquisition of stockbrokerage Hoare Govett in London was an innovative step well before the onset of Big Bang made such acquisitions the flavor of the month, but in late 1988 the problems of dealing with different cultures as well as a drop in transaction volume have turned this initiative into an albatross in the minds of many observers of the London scene. To quote one of these observers:

People remain skeptical of the strategy. They're still performing well in terms of their peer group, but they're going off in a lot of different directions, and there are problems in Arizona and Hoare Govett. We're concerned about focus; they could be a dominant West Coast bank. Has their strategy been put together in too rapid a fashion?

Echoes another panelist:

> **What are they trying to do? They botched Big Bang in
> London. They've blown hot and cold in their wholesale
> business. Even in California they haven't developed
> the retail and middle market thrust they should have.
> There's a surprising inconsistency.**

The public image of Sumitomo Bank has also suffered
from outsiders' doubts about strategic initiatives. While
Credit Suisse has skyrocketed in bankologists' esteem by
their acquisition of effective control of a major New York
investment bank, Sumitomo has lost face by acquiring for
$500 million a non-voting minority position in another,
Goldman Sachs, and not even benefitted from the transfer
of experience which was the avowed goal of the exercise.

Another perspective on winners and losers can be gained
by analyzing the newcomers to the excellence rolls. S.G.
Warburg is technically not a newcomer in that the number
of votes it received – pre-merger – in 1984 were arbitrarily
disqualified by the author on the basis of the previous,
narrower definition of 'bank'. Its attraction to the majority
of our panel in 1988 stemmed not only from its strong
leadership role among British merchant banks but also its
successful four-way merger prior to Big Bang.

In sharp contrast to its merchant banking peers as well as
commercial banks such as Barclays and National Westminster
Bank, Warburg, as we have seen in earlier chapters, managed
to link different cultures, information technologies and
product strengths with a minimal loss of customers and
key staffers. It faces an uphill struggle in its declared goal
of becoming a global investment bank with local strength
in New York as well as Tokyo, but at a minimum Warburg
is deemed by London observers to have an almost unas-
sailable grip on the leadership sweepstakes in London
among British-owned institutions.

A second entrant to the excellent rolls in 1988 has been
National Westminster Bank. In its dual with Barclays for
the top slot in the performance race, NatWest bested
its rival in the late 1980s on most statistical performance
measures. Superior credit quality, performance in the vital

US market and a strategic focus on the highly profitable UK market lay behind this superior performance.

While NatWest was often damned with faint praise by being cited as having made fewer mistakes than its British peers - particularly in sovereign risk lending – its halo was tarnished in 1988 by the well-publicized problems associated with its investment banking subsidiary. For many panelists the substantial financial losses posted in 1987-88 by NatWest Investment Bank and the cultural turmoil associated with them constituted a substantial negative factor. But for most, these were seen to be manageable and not significantly more serious than those of Barclays.

The final newcomer to the excellent list is PNC Financial, whose praises were sung in the quotation by one of our panelists on p.5. PNC received a few votes in 1984, but its rise in voting strength is largely attributable to its perceived mastery of the interstate banking scene in the US. Without the incumbus of a major burden of LDC debt, PNC has been among the leaders in exploiting the gradual removal of interstate banking barriers. Such mastery is attributed by our panel to strong leadership, striking a positive balance between preserving local relationships and developing central controls, augmenting product volume rather than slashing payrolls, and concentrating on product strengths which provide a strategic competitive advantage.

Having now reviewed our findings in the two sets of interviews as well as interrogated our panelists once again, what conclusions do we draw as to the factors which separate the banks on the current excellent list from their peers? How useful were the conclusions of *Excellence in Banking*? And how relevant are the four key success factors elaborated in this volume?

The first conclusion is that the ten characteristics of excellent banks in 1984 are of only marginal value in selecting winners in an environment of rapid change. They describe traits which can legitimately be claimed by a host of banking institutions. This does not detract from their value as standards of performance or planning goals, but they are not sharp enough to separate winners from losers in a world overfilled with banking institutions engaged in a war of attrition.

Perhaps the best analogy is that of entrance into a coveted hall of higher learning. The frustrated parent of a bright child applying for entrance into the likes of Tokyo University, Amherst College, Oxford University or the Ecole Nationale d'Administration quickly becomes aware that his offspring meets the technical requirements for entrance in terms of native intelligence, yet some choice must be made to reduce the resulting qualifying entrants by a factor of four or five to fit the number of available places. Such a second cut is made on different criteria: extra-curricular achievement, a special examination, or political influence.

In this context, the worth of the four success factors analyzed in Chapters 7 through 10 is confirmed. While the difficulty in applying rigorous qualification standards in the selection process must temper any conclusions, the panelists in their judgements did substantiate the importance of critical mass, the choice of strategic direction, the ability to manage diversity, and the creation of a meritocracy.

Critical mass, for example, is the starting point for most bankologists. Whether by luck or judgement, does the banking institution have an attractive core business base, or can it acquire one by acquisition or organic growth? Threatened with the loss of its Hong Kong franchise, HongkongBank has successfully diversified by acquisition and strategic stakes into the US and UK. In contrast, Bank of Tokyo is perceived by many to have been left in the dust. J.P. Morgan, Bankers Trust and Citicorp all faced the loss of their core franchise – wholesale banking – and responded either by building a retail banking franchise or using product advantage to enter the securities business.

Security Pacific is seen by many panelists to be in danger of losing its critical mass in the home base of Southern California in favor of adventures abroad. In contrast, First Wachovia chose its merger partner in Georgia to achieve critical mass in that key market. Faced with the daunting competition outside its home base in Bavaria, Bayerische Vereinsbank has understandably preferred to avoid dilution of its resources and remain a regional institution.

The related issue of strategy also emerges unscathed from this introspection. While the old saw about success being 10 per cent strategy and 90 per cent implementation has a great deal of truth, the 90 per cent effort may be largely wasted if the 10 per cent of forward thinking does not provide a potential strategic advantage. Arguably this may account for the absence of any Japanese banks from the excellence list in 1988. The Japanese City banks, with the possible exception of Sumitomo Bank, are still travelling in tight strategic convoy despite years of gradual deregulation. The minimum of strategic differentiation in a world which has gone in the other direction must pose problems for the future

The remarkable transformation of Citicorp from an international wholesale bank in 1979 to one today largely dependent on retail earnings is a tribute to exceptional strategic vision. Bankers Trust and Morgan Guaranty over the same period have become accepted players in the global securities business from a standing start. HongkongBank is another which has set out on a determined path to transform itself from a regional bank serving the Chinese retail community in Asia into a global business with strength in key capital and commercial banking markets in Europe and the US.

In the global investment banking market, strategic choice in a deregulating environment has been a particularly critical differentiating factor during the 1980s. Despite clear historical patterns of boom and bust in the business of underwriting and distributing securities outside national markets, a host of national institutions with domestic origination or distribution power were attracted like moths to a flame by a combination of national deregulation and favorable trends in interest rates and equity prices in the mid-1980s. Big Bang in London in 1986 was the best publicized of the resulting massive increases in capacity, but similar explosions occurred in the Pacific Basin and Continental Europe.

The resulting rush of securities firms to go global without serious consideration of the consequences of similar strategies of their peers ressembled, as Hans-Joerg Rudloff points out, the lemming-like expansion which has characterized their commercial banking brethren. In London, it took a brave management decision for a merchant bank like Schroders or Barings to opt out of the international securities sweepstakes when conventional wisdom dictated that their traditional corporate finance and other core businesses would be lost to the big battalions if they did not acquire an integrated securities research, trading and distribution capability. In the perspective of late 1988, their decision to focus on their strengths was the envy of others like Morgan Grenfell faced with a painful and expensive shrinking of capacity.

Among the banking institutions which dropped from the excellent list for this volume are several which have been unable to capitalize on domestic securities strengths such as corporate relationships or placing power to build a corresponding capability in the international markets. Japanese banks such as Bank of Tokyo and Sumitomo Bank have not been able to position themselves among the leaders, while S-E-Banken has remained largely focussed on Scandinavian securities. Bayerische Vereinsbank is a major factor in DM-denominated securities, yet Deutsche Bank has been able to work its way to the top of the global league tables almost regardless of the currency involved.

Yet it is the management of diversity implied by successful expansion into new geographic and product markets which has most sharply separated the winners and losers during the second half of the 1980s. It is one thing to acknowledge, as all of our excellent banks have done in this book, that one cannot impose one's own culture on a foreign unit doing business with local customers. It is quite another to allow this culture in practice to be diluted by the extent of delegation which is implied in the real banking world. For head office to suspend judgement on local credit, systems and people decisions is a gut-wrenching choice – particularly for a Continental European or Japanese bank which prides itself on a centralized, highly structured decision-making process.

The agony is particularly difficult for Japanese banks. A friend at Sumitomo Bank, which made one of the first Japanese bank acquisitions early in the 1980s when it bought Banco Del Gottardo, confirms the dilemma:

We're tightly controlled, tightly managed; it makes it difficult to manage an acquisition. We'd have to change our culture to achieve it. We'd lose our strength. We can leave Gottardo as is – it's small enough.

The same theme is echoed in conversations with senior management at Swiss Bank Corporation, Deutsche Bank and National Westminster Bank. A small acquisition, preferably of a specialist organization which can continue to operate on its own without requiring change in the parent, is acceptable. But a major acquisition – much less a merger of equals – which requires cultural change throughout the organization is approached with great trepidation.

In this context, the achievement of HongkongBank, First Wachovia, PNC Financial and S.G. Warburg in successfully managing the transformation of their businesses through the acquisition process is a signal one. And Citicorp's ability to manage the diversity of roughly 100 businesses around the globe, despite the level of conflict which accompanies it, is absolutely unique. One can understand the reluctance of a Bayerische Vereinsbank or Sumitomo Bank to risk diluting its strengths by attempting to incorporate different cultures. And one can appreciate the skepticism of analysts concerned about Security Pacific's ability to manage its profusion of non-banking interests.

Another dimension of our third criterion of management skills relates to the embarrassing gaffes highlighted by our panelists in their evaluation process. A major fraud loss, malfunctioning of control systems or undue risk concentration can happen – and has – to the best of our excellent banks, but hopefully less often than with peers without effective management controls. And it is during today's environment of rapid change that management processes are tested to the limit.

Finally, our fourth success factor – attracting and retaining the best people through a culture of meritocracy – has been confirmed by the experience of the past few years. It was acknowledged in many of the ten traits of excellent institutions in the first volume: a commitment to recruit the best people, investing in training, and a strong and consistent leadership. Credit Suisse First Boston, J.P. Morgan, Citicorp, Deutsche Bank and their excellent peers are still regarded as being able to attract the best talent in the business.

But as banking emerges from the shackles of a regulated industry and sells its expertise rather than credit capacity or traditional franchise, banking products are increasingly equated with people skills. A client goes to Citicorp for a foreign exchange solution or Credit Suisse First Boston to place a particular type of security for their acknowledged human skills, not their balance sheet size.

And this product leadership brings us back to the issue of innovation and entrepreneurship which in *Excellence in Banking* constituted the principal barrier between the non-bank institutions of *In Search of Excellence* and our sample of excellent banks in 1984. People will increasingly become the differentiating factor among banking institutions as product differentiation increases in a competitive world.

Comparing the excellent lists in 1984 and 1988 for such qualities as people quality and innovation is an impossible task given the difficulty of defining such intangible traits. Yet the various customer polls which evaluate attitudes towards financial intermediaires in the capital market and other sectors repeatedly give pride of place to institutions like CSFB, J.P. Morgan, Bankers Trust and Citicorp in key product areas. In late 1988, for example, the *Euromoney* magazine poll of banking competitors elected Bankers Trust and J.P. Morgan, respectively, the most innovative firms in the Eurobond and Euronote/Euroloan markets.

Before concluding our comparison of the two excellent lists, however, several points should be made. First, the distance which separates those which fell from grace in 1988 and those remaining on the list is both short and variable in nature. As we pointed out in *Excellence in Banking*, each bank is a mosaic of strengths and weaknesses. Honest observers of the banking scene can usually honestly agree on these variables. The difficulty comes in the admittedly subjective weighting of these strengths and weaknesses in producing an overall appraisal for the short list we requested.

Thus even some of the banks with the highest number of panel votes came in for some less than ebullient comments. Even the Vorstand members of Deutsche Bank interviewed in 1988 implicitly agree with some of the market comments about the bank's slowness in making strategic decisions and the likely difficulty of making the cultural change to a truly multinational bank.

J.P. Morgan, virtually every panelist's choice in 1988, has admittedly gone through a difficult period in the late 1980s in reconciling its traditional strengths with a performance culture. As one of our panelists explains:

They're less distinctly superior than four years ago. They've had problems managing change and diversity as seen from the client's point of view. The halo has been crafted over generations and it's still there, but it's tarnished.

And what about Citicorp, which *Excellence in Banking* awarded the accolade of the banking institution which came closest to meeting the eight traits of the winners in *In Search of Excellence?* Its success in managing — and welcoming — diverse cultures, innovating in product development and executing a successful strategic switch to retail banking insure Citicorp's inclusion in almost any list of superior banks as well as ranking in the top handful of institutions measured on our four critical success factors.[2] But listen to one of our panelists, who articulates a commonly-held view:

Citicorp has sinned in its failure to understand the importance of consistency. They've embraced change but done it in a child-like fashion. Their execution is barely satisfactory. But you can't conclude that their strategy is wrong. They think strategically.

And the scrupulously honest Citibankers agree. Referring to the bank's investment banking business in the late 1980s, Michael Callen, its investment banking head, admits:

Two years ago we shouldn't have sounded so sure. We did some dumb things. We were guilty of overstating the case.[2]

As we pointed out earlier in this chapter, many panelists questioned on their deletion of banks from the 1984 list admitted on reflection that the quality of management of those dropped had not deteriorated. Thus Swiss Bank Corporation, Bayerische Vereinsbank and Barclays Bank lost votes but not the esteem of the voters. In such cases others, in their view, such as National Westminster, Credit Suisse and PNC Financial had shown superior ability to master the challenges of the current environment.

A second conclusion from this exercise is that timing is a critical variable in the selection of any list of superior institutions. Two factors lie behind this caveat. One is that panelists' views are inevitably skewed by recent headlines –

which may or may not reflect underlying excellence. In late 1988, such recent events include National Westminster's current investment banking problems, Swiss Bank Corporation's embarrassment with the Coop group in Germany, Union Bank of Switzerland's integration of the stockbrokerage Phillips and Drew, and Deutsche Bank's apparent coup in acquiring Banca d'America e d'Italia in anticipation of 1992.

A more fundamental difficulty in taking a photograph as we have at four year intervals is that reasoned conclusions on the value of many strategic initiatives can require a decade or more of experience to validate. Were one to appraise Citicorp's US retail initiative in the early 1980s when its fixed rate loan portfolio was being funded at negative interest rates due to statutory rate ceilings, the answer would have been muted at best.

A current case in point is that of Sumitomo Bank, which lost many votes in 1988 because of the apparent setbacks in the Goldman Sachs and Heiwa Sogo initiatives described earlier. But when can one draw the line under them? The comments of our friend at Sumitomo Bank echo the question marks in the minds of many of our panelists:

> **We're in a stage of transformation. Ten years ago we weren't a top name like Mitsubishi Bank. Now we're a contender. We're not yet the champion, but we're getting there. As for Goldman Sachs and Heiwa Sogo, the important thing is it was we who took the initiative in each case. We don't know yet whether they were the right initiatives, but as long as we retain the capability to take initiatives in the Japanese context, I'm sure we'll become the real champion.**

Another case in point is the duel between Barclays and National Westminster Bank for leadership in the UK. Stung by its earnings problems in the mid-1980s, Barclays has surged since then in the view of many London observers. At the end of 1988, the growing reputation of its securities affiliate BZW was overshadowing NatWest's performance in building NatWest Investment Bank. To many observers, the outcome of this duel is still in doubt.

Having now planted our flag in a world of banking change by choosing our four key success factors, we can conclude this final chapter with a few observations as to what the future may hold for the excellent banks which emerge successfully from the shoot-out of the 1990s. Chapter 10 looked at the structural issues such as the extent of likely concentration in the sector. What about the profile of individual excellent banking institutions?

The first conclusion is that there will be relatively few institutions with the skills to manage successfully a range of diverse businesses and cultures. Citicorp, with all of its financial and human resources, has showed how difficult it is to manage diversity even with its espoused goal of a meritocracy, non-Americans in a variety of senior positions and strong franchises in a variety of attractive national markets. It may be a problem of physical size, or leadership continuity, or perhaps inherent in the nature of a personal services business. Whatever the cause, many of our panelists are disappointed with the result. Even J.P. Morgan, with its tenacious commitment to a Morgan culture, is finding it difficult to achieve the right balance between traditional culture and profit maximization in the securities business.

And what about the others? Fanciful projections of pan-European banks in the context of 1992 seem unrealistic in the face of the lack of real progress to date by European banks in achieving the necessary melding of cultures and decentralization they acknowledge is necessary to achieve this ideal. It is one thing for Deutsche Bank or Sumitomo Bank to acquire a well-run affiliate abroad and leave it to its own devices. It is something quite different to make them responsive elements of a truly multinational, coordinated strategy.

In London, Swiss Bank Corporation is physically merging its stockbrokerage, investment banking and commercial banking arms. Union Bank of Switzerland hopes to merge British stockbrokers and Swiss investment bankers in a decentralized environment. They may well succeed, but one doubts whether many others will.

Managing diversity brings one back to Dick Thomson's point about banking being a local business – and the local bankers' business being to keep it that way in the face of competition from foreign interlopers. Product range and quality, well supported by strong leadership, high quality local people and the willingness to delegate to these people can go a long way to offsetting loyalties to traditional suppliers. But we are not sanguine on the basis of the experience of the past decade that many can provide this offset.

The problem is one of achieving a delicate balance in not just one but a multiplicity of dimensions. In the domain of risk, we have seen that a system of checks and balances is essential. Balancing the natural desire to undertake a profitable transaction or respond quickly to a client need must be reconciled with an understanding of the risk involved and possible risk concentration.

In blending cultures in a diverse business, management must find the right balance on the one hand between local initiative and circumstance and, on the other, bank-wide tenets such as communication and loyalty to the customer. In setting strategy, it must be both bold in setting itself apart from the competition, and conservative in not betting the bank should things go wrong. Finally, in that most sensitive domain of incentive compensation, management must find the right blend between rewarding individual initiative and commitment to the institution.

The demands thus posed on top management in a fast-moving world to find the right point of equilibrium in all these areas will test the wisdom of Solomon. Faced with complicating their task even further by major expansion through mergers and significant new product areas, we believe most bank managements will opt for focussing their efforts on businesses and markets they know best.

We thus see sharper focus on markets in which banks have achieved critical mass and have some form of competitive advantage. As the Cooke Committee's capital adequacy guidelines bite deeper, it will become harder to justify major initiatives outside these geographic or product markets. This does not necessarily mean an ebbing of the tide of physical expansion outside traditional borders. But the retreat of North American banks from their overseas networks is a phenomenon which may be repeated by others hard pressed to meet capital adequacy standards.

As excellent banks are deterred by the problems of managing diversity from penetrating new markets, they will find real opportunities for strategic development in their core businesses. Their American peers have shown what can be done. At one extreme is to leave the banking business entirely in the sense of taking deposits and making loans – in favor of selling expertise in the form of financial advice or data processing systems. Others will essentially become distributors of banking and non-banking products through their unique branch distribution networks.

The strategic dilemma is perhaps sharpest for banks which have taken full advantage of such opportunities in their home markets yet still feel compelled to expand outside in one form or another. Product-driven expansion is an option – but only for those who have invested in the people skills necessary to obtain a competitive advantage. Building a core business in new markets through organic growth has been eschewed by most as being too time consuming and risky. Even in the context of European integration in 1992, banks like National Westminster and Deutsche Bank which have built strong domestic networks are reluctant to replicate this process abroad.

What remains is therefore the acquisition route for those with the valuation ratios which permit them to buy businesses at minimum cost to their own market valuation and the skills to manage diversity. Thus National Australia Bank, one of the top three in the competitive Australian market, has purchased three retail banking businesses in Scotland and Ireland at minimal cost to its earnings per share in its first major venture outside Australia.

Whatever the strategy, the four success factors articulated in this book will remain relevant. The overwhelming challenge for banking leadership will be to achieve a positive balance between entrepreneurship and stability, individual initiative and benefit to the group, and the trade-off between individual and common cultural norms within a single organization.

Notes and References

2   Risk: Some New Dimensions

1. Banking World (May 1988).

4   Managing Technology

1. *Banking World* (May 1988).
2. *Forbes Magazine* (25 April 1988).

5   Managing Different Cultures

1. *International Finance Review* (2 January 1988).

6   Strategy: Competitive Advantage in an Uncertain World

1. *Wall St Journal* (22 March 1988).
2. *Chief Executive* (September/October 1987).

8   People: Towards the Global Meritocracy

1. *The Economist* (7th May 1988).
2. *Banking world* (May 1988).
3. *Institutional Investor* (November 1985).

9   The Management Factor

1. *American Banker* (8 September 1987).
2. *Euromoney* (September 1987).
3. *Banking World* (May 1988).

11   Banking Excellence Revisited: Winners and Losers in an Environment of Competition and Change

1. *Euromoney* (September 1988).
2. *Institutional Investor* (December 1988).

Index of Bankers

Index of Subjects